I DO?

Being Happy Being Married

Lee Schnebly

FISHER BOOKS

Publishers: Helen V. Fisher
Howard W. Fisher
Fred W. Fisher
E. Thomas Monroe

Art Director: Josh Young

Published by Fisher Books
3499 N. Campbell Avenue
Suite 909
Tucson, Arizona 85719
(602) 325-5263

**Library of Congress
Cataloging-in-publication Data**

Schnebly, Lee, 1932-
I do?

Includes index.
1. Communication in marriage.
2. Marriage —United States—Psy-
chological aspects. I. Title.
HQ734.S388 1988 646.7'8 88-24594
ISBN 1-55561-016-1 (pbk.)

Fisher Books are available at
special quantity discounts for edu-
cational use. Special books, or
book excerpts, can also be
created to fit specific needs. For
details please write or telephone.

Books by

Lee Schnebly:

Out of Apples?

Do-It-Yourself Happiness

I Do?

Dedication

To all the people who started out as
clients and ended up as friends.

CONTENTS

About the Author

Lee Schnebly is a certified mental-health counselor in Tucson, Arizona, specializing in marriage, family and individual counseling. Her warm, lighthearted style makes her a popular author and speaker. Her speeches and books make you feel refreshed and uplifted.

Lee's prior books are *Out of Apples?* and *Do-It-Yourself Happiness.* In them you will find additional encouragement and discover what makes you happy.

Lee invites you to enjoy life to the fullest!

Chapter 1

They Do

I love weddings. Each one to which we're invited gives me weeks of pleasant anticipation. When the day finally arrives I like to get there early enough to get a good seat. I want to relish the sight of each bridesmaid proceeding up the aisle to music that implies something important. I delight in watching the ushers walk purposefully front and center. The groom stands watching for the first sight of his beloved. And when the bride herself appears in all her splendor, I can hardly stand it! Inevitably my throat closes and I struggle to choke back tears of emotion as I watch father and daughter march bravely and proudly toward the altar.

As I watch the pageant, I puzzle about my overwhelming response of emotion. Maybe these tears are the same kind that can well up at a parade when the band is playing something powerfully majestic, with flags being raised by proud young scouts and excited majorettes flashing batons with practiced skill. The mood is positive, full of hope and promise. It's the ideal of what we like to expect; that life is good and people are participating in a splendid ceremony symbolizing the good that is to follow.

In a wedding, the same elements of pomp and ceremony entertain us, and in addition we get to re-ex-
perience the dream of how love should be. We do know
how love should be. Watching a wedding seems kind of
like watching a marvelous preview of the coming lifetime
of love and happiness.

Surely *this* bride and groom, as excitedly happy as they
look, can continue living their lives in this cloud of love.
Look at the expressions on their young faces as they repeat the vows! Just hear the earnestness in their voices as
they say, "I do." They really mean it!

Those of us watching may reflect on our own marriages. Sometimes we determine again to make happen the
promises we once made at our own weddings.

At the same time, there are likely to be a few cynics in
the congregation. But even their skepticism is the result
of having been disappointed in dreams of perfected love.
And there are also a few observers (usually the very
young) who buy the whole package hook, line and
sinker, with never a doubt that the newlyweds will live
perfectly happily ever after.

But probably the most emotion wells up in those of us
who fall between those two categories. We're neither ardent believers nor cynical nonbelievers. We *want* to
believe in the joyful future of these two people, but we're
a little afraid to. We did once, and we've been burned.

We want to warn this couple so they can avoid getting
burned. We want to say, "Wait, dear young people! You're
so young and so inexperienced and so vulnerable . . .
what you're doing today is such an enormous step you
can't possibly comprehend it! We're talking *For Life,* here.
Commitment of the most mammoth proportions! See,
there are so many things you don't realize. It's going to be
so much *hard work!*"

In spite of the hard work, we don't want them *not* to marry. We see the love and admiration on their faces, and we want them to have the experience of joy that marriage can provide. We want them to know the delight of sleeping in on Sunday mornings and reading the paper together over cinnamon rolls and coffee. We want them to have each other available to listen to stories of what they endured during the day. They can enjoy life so much more fully with a mate beside them who really knows and understands them. They might even get to share the birth of a child and the bonding joy that experience can bring. Even the nights walking a colicky baby should be shared, as should the pride of seeing that baby graduate from high school.

What a wonderful opportunity they have, we think. We might even want to say, "Look, you two. *Appreciate this!* This can be the start of something so wonderful that nothing else in life can compare. You can make this work! It's a challenge, but you can conquer it if you do the right things. It's all in your hands."

Maybe it's all these thoughts and feelings welling up inside us that can't help but cause a tear or two. Maybe our own projection of old dreams, hurts, joys, disillusionments and hopes whirl with such intensity in our heads that we can't possibly separate the good from the bad.

But the bride and groom rarely have such doubts. They are able to say, "I do," with such sincerity and such naiveté that we happily give them our blessings. We want nothing but the best for them as we stand in the reception line waiting to give them both a hug, toast them, share their cake, give them gifts and watch them drive away to a new life full of promise and expectation.

But deep down inside we wonder if they could possibly know what they just said when they said, "I do."

Certainly they meant it, but did they comprehend it? I believe no one comprehends it at that stage in life.

To begin with, two people who have fallen in love are in no condition to make any kind of important decision. They can barely function on any level, so out of their heads in love are they. Rational? Logical? No way. Completely helpless is more like it.

Scientists have studied people in love, trying to pinpoint the physical manifestations the love bug brings. They have found there are actual chemical changes that affect us in many ways.

Most of these are positive. We bloom. We look and feel better than we have in the past. We get by with a minimum of food and sleep, and yet we feel like we could move mountains. The behavior we exhibit is often manic. Euphoric. Excited. We're totally optimistic and ready to tackle anything. So heady are these feelings that falling in love renders us emotionally unstable.

We might almost be labeled temporarily insane. And it's in that wacky, unstable state of near insanity that we make perhaps the biggest decision in our lives—to marry.

Is there any hope for a marriage that was made by two people in that atmosphere? Absolutely.

Then why are there so many unhappily married people?

Because nobody ever taught us *how* to be married. All we had to learn from was watching the way our parents did it, and usually we determined *not* to do it their way!

This book will provide some ideas about how to be married that may be different from some you've tried. I believe they'll help make your marriage better. If I practice what I preach, they'll make *mine* better as well!

The Marriage Counselor's Marriage

I want to make a confession here and now. Mine is not a perfect marriage.

Some people may assume that marriage counselors have the process down to a perfected skill, but alas, 'tis not so. Priests, ministers and rabbis are still known to sin occasionally. Physicians get sick. Models gain weight and/or get zits. Bridges designed by brilliant engineers have been known to crack or collapse. All of those happenings are a normal part of life.

Don't believe I have achieved perfection in marriage, because it simply is not true. It's not even possible. Though I'd like to be able to blame my husband ("I could have a perfect marriage if he'd just shape up"), I must confess to making a sizeable contribution to an imperfect relationship myself. Not deliberately, but the result is still the same: disappointment on both sides.

Occasionally someone tells me, "We have a marvelous marriage. We've never fought or argued in 20 years." I always smile and say, "How nice for you!" Inwardly I suspect there are flies in the ointment that both people have chosen to pretend don't exist.

Perhaps there are a few good souls who were blessed with mates who match or complement their own personalities. But if even *near* perfection prevails it's a rare and glorious happening. Most of us have to work very very very hard to keep a relationship rewarding to both parties.

I know that people sometimes think Larry's and my marriage is one of those made-in-Heaven love nests, because we usually look relatively content. In a way it's almost too bad that most of us do walk around looking content, because we perpetuate the myth that we've got it all together. That makes the rest of us feel sorry for ourselves because we know "our marriage isn't as good as most people's."

Larry and I will no doubt continue looking like Mr. and Mrs. Perfect for social occasions, but I want to publicly announce that we don't always act like that at home. There have been times that we've argued all the way to a party, argued as we went up the walk and rang the doorbell, and as the host opened the door we both beamed merrily and sang a happy, "Hi!" We looked calm and pleasant all during cocktails and dinner, actually did enjoy ourselves, said warm thanks and good-byes to our host and hostess, and resumed hostilities on our way back to the car.

I believe that is typical. It doesn't happen to us too often, thank goodness, but often enough to keep me humble as a marriage counselor. About the time I get too big for my britches and think I've got all the answers, we reach another major glitch in our relationship. There is more stress and pain and anxiety while we work through still another difference of opinion.

It no longer frightens me, however. It's kind of like the flu. Now and then you get it. You feel feverish and rotten and discouraged and helpless, but if you hang in there and take good care of yourself you recover sooner or later. You would never *want* it, but it's a part of life that seems to be unavoidable.

When I feel miffed and vexed with Larry, I can accept the bad feelings the way I do a sore throat. It doesn't signal danger, but it does demand that attention be paid to it. Just like a cold, a marriage needs special care when it's sick.

Many times that fact in itself irritates us. We don't *want* to have to deal with a sick marriage; we just want it to stay well. Of course it *would* stay well if we took good care of it in the first place, but we usually neglect it.

Perhaps we have to suffer discomfort in order to learn. Certainly, I grew up hearing my mother say that vegetables are good for us, sweets aren't, etc., etc. As soon as I hit junior high I rejected most of her advice and stuffed myself with candy bars and doughnuts after breakfasting on fudge and cola. Of course I got fat and pimply and miserable and hated myself. You'd think I would have changed my eating habits immediately, wouldn't you? But instead I continued trying to beat the system for many years, wanting to eat all the things I craved, but avoid the consequences. Now, in my fifties, it seems so simple. It just isn't worth the price to eat sweet things and feel the sugar highs that turn to lows. Drinking more than one glass of wine makes me dopey, so why do it? I eat giant salads that Mama would have been thrilled to see, and I've learned to love them.

All of that gives me continued hope about marriage. I'm coming to terms with the reality that if I want a blissful state I have to do something to achieve it. You can't

beat the system. A "happily-ever-after" marriage will
never *just happen.*

Marriage is probably the biggest challenge we face in
life. In my opinion it needs more thought, care, attention
and energy than most other jobs we take on. "Jobs?" Even
as I type the word something in me feels jarred. "Jobs"
sounds suspiciously like work.

Am I putting marriage in the same category as cleaning the bathroom? Taking out the trash? Putting in an
eight-hour day at the stock market? Building a house?

Yep. And perhaps that is part of the problem. Most of
us went into marriage with the expectation that it would
be the fun that *followed* the hard work; not more hard
work in itself. We're twice as disillusioned when we must
come to terms with a state of life that is no longer much
fun at all.

But I don't want to imply that marriage is only as rewarding as taking out the trash. I truly do believe it can
be the most rewarding occupation in the whole world. It
has to be considered a responsibility that requires con-
sistent attention if it's going to fly. It can and should be
fun in the process.

After all, there are jobs and there are jobs. I can't pretend I'd love spending eight hours a day cooking hamburgers. But would I love being activities director on a
cruise ship? You bet! Would it be fun to be a movie star
and work with Robert Redford? I hope to tell you it would!

Probably even cruise-ship personnel find their jobs
tiresome from time to time. Having to work up enthusiasm for touring Puerto Vallarta would get to be a drag after
you've done it enough times, as would all the other details
of being responsible for other people's happiness.

Could it be that I'd even tire of doing love scenes with
Robert Redford? Now *that* I doubt, but I know I'd hate

having to get up at four in the morning to do it. Friends who work as extras in the movies at Old Tucson complain of endless boring hours waiting in the 110-degree sun. We who don't make our living that way can't comprehend the trials connected with film making that make it hard work.

Nevertheless, many people in the business enjoy it. Work *can* be joyful. You just know that it won't be all fun, and you prepare your expectations accordingly. I would hope that even if I had to cook hamburgers all day, I could find some fun in it while I worked toward goals that would land me a better job.

The process of work gives us a sense of self-worth. Alfred Adler used to say, "Work is worth." To have nothing to work at would be demeaning and destructive to one's self-image.

Which means that acknowledging marriage as work isn't necessarily unpleasant. Once we recognize it as a task-oriented process, we can tackle it with enthusiasm and make it satisfy us in so many ways.

Is it for everyone?

Not in a million years. Some people should avoid it like the plague. Folks who put a high priority on independence and autonomy might never be willing to pay the price of constantly working together. Many of us should also avoid taking jobs as cruise-ship directors or movie stars, because we're not temperamentally suited for people-involved positions. We might make better architects, engineers, artists, computer analysts or composers, fields that don't demand a lot of interpersonal relating. That doesn't make us faulty or lacking or wrong. In fact it indicates we have the wisdom to know ourselves, to know what we like and don't like, what we're good at and not so good at.

Society has made marriage almost a "given" for so long

that lots of people choose it because they think it's expected of them. They know no other way. That is becoming less true today, as we see more singles living alone than ever before. I think it's marvelous that we're coming to see marriage as an option rather than a necessity.

It's a necessity only if we want to have children, and some people even disagree with me on that score.

It's too bad that we generally can't figure all this out long before we reach the age of marrying, because it might prevent some of us from jumping into a way of life that is totally inappropriate. But given the "insanity" that overtakes us when we fall in love, we often couldn't make a wise, well-thought-out decision if we tried.

So let's say we're married. We got married way back when we were young and foolish (or old and foolish) and thought it was going to be great, marvelous fun living with this perfect mate.

Now we're disillusioned. It's anything but fun. It's a drag. We're both disappointed and discouraged. The starry-eyed expectations have turned into a living hell. Can this be how marriage is supposed to be? Do other married couples feel this low down? Surely not. If I am married and so unhappy I must have an unhappy marriage, right?

Not necessarily. In fact, *probably* not. In most cases it's a matter of mistaken beliefs and expectations that didn't materialize. Most of the time the relationship can be vastly improved. That is the purpose of this book.

I meant it when I said that if I practice what I preach it will even help *my* marriage. Much of the time there's nothing wrong with an institution or a process; it's just that the people involved are doing it incorrectly. I find that immensely encouraging. I can change my behavior if it's going to make me happier.

I was heartened a few weeks ago when I confided to our son Lyle that, "Dad and I are having problems again," and heard his response. Lyle (24 and married) said confidently, "As long as you guys keep trying it'll be okay. Just don't quit trying, that's all."

I saw the confidence in his eyes and gave him an appreciative hug. He's right, of course. (How did this little kid get so smart?!)

It's never going to be *easy* improving our relationship. Larry and I are so different in so many ways, it's downright remarkable we get along at all! I know he suffers as much as I do from time to time.

But both of us are committed to our relationship and we'll keep hanging in there until we improve things. With two people constantly changing and growing— frequently in opposite directions—it's an enormous challenge to keep readjusting the dynamics of living together.

I'm always the one saying, "We've got a problem. We need to talk." He rolls his eyes and looks to the heavens pleadingly as if to say, "Not again, Lord. Make her stop."

But I am relentless. I never stop, at least not for long. And I know he doesn't really want me to stop because if we ever stop, the marriage is doomed. We want this marriage.

When Larry and I met 39 years ago, I wouldn't have dreamed that our marriage would ever require any work. We were madly in love; our song was "Tenderly;" our future would surely be nothing but bliss. Now I'm older and wiser. I know there are times when our marriage needs work.

Chapter 3

Where's the Contract?

If I had to identify the biggest cause of marital unhappiness I'd say it's the set of expectations we have about marriage in the first place.

Each of us has generally had some 20 to 30 years to formulate our beliefs as to what marriage should be like, and we think we know what to expect when we finally make the commitment. Whether we want to emulate the relationship we saw between our parents, or whether we want to completely avoid interaction like theirs, we have definite ideas about how marriage should be.

Here is where we get in trouble. It would be different if we went shopping for a spouse the way we shop for a car. We have definite likes and dislikes, and most of us take quite a lot of time searching for the one car that comes closest to fulfilling all our wishes.

We consider price, appearance, mileage, brands and optional equipment. Regardless of our budget we usually shop carefully. If we buy from the classified ads, we interview the seller and take the car to our trusted mechanic for a checkup. If we buy from a dealer, we consider his reputation as well as that of the manufacturer.

When I bought my last car I knew *exactly* what features I wanted and how much I could spend. I stood firm on all the items I wanted, shopping at several dealers until I found the one that had what I could afford in a car that met most of my requirements. Even then I questioned the salesman lengthily about warranties and service. By the time I drove the car home I knew precisely what I was getting and what kind of performance I could expect. We'd signed a contract with everything down in black and white. It had been an interaction based on logical communication, facts, figures and legalities.

Marriage? It's just about as opposite as can be.

Oh, there are *some* similarities, to be sure. In both cars and spouses we have firm ideas as to what we want and how we expect them to perform for us. But that is where the similarities end.

In choosing mates we let our emotions, rather than facts and logic, guide us. We don't make a considered decision. We fall in love when we least expect it.

"Now I believe in love at first sight."

"When he came into the restaurant I said to another waitress, 'There's my future husband.'"

"The first time I met her I was turned off completely, but the second time I knew she was the one I wanted to grow old with."

"My kids loved her, and I knew she'd be a good mother to them."

"It was during the war. I was to ship out the next week, so we eloped after knowing each other for just two weeks."

"He reminded me of Jimmy Dean."

It's fun to hear our reasons for deciding to marry. Granted, a few people take plenty of time in deciding, but most of us don't take nearly enough time. We willingly and eagerly jump feet-first into a lifelong commitment without ever thinking, *buyer beware*. The only warranty we get is, "Till death do us part."

Would anyone in his right mind buy a car like that?

Imagine seeing a car with a FOR SALE sign in its window and deciding that *that* is the car we'll drive for the rest of our lives because it's such a neat shade of blue. Although it's a ridiculous thought, it isn't unlike many of our reasons for marrying.

But let's say we're smarter than the average person. We've taken a lot of time to think about our needs in marriage. We've "shopped around" for years and gotten to know what the opposite sex is all about. We've dated dozens, rejected and been rejected. We've become so wise and discerning we can spot the potential problems in a relationship within the first couple of dates.

And one day we meet Mr. Perfect or Ms. Perfect. Warily we begin to let ourselves think, "Maybe this time . . ."

We agree on total honesty. We talk endlessly and discover more and more similarities. We come from the same socioeconomic backgrounds. Our spiritual beliefs are compatible. We laugh a lot and enjoy the same activities. We both (or neither) want children. We even agree on wanting to live in the same city forever. Our families like each other. The physical attraction between us is nothing short of fireworks and Disneyland. Wow, this is *it* . . . this is really *it!* We've been together now for a year and now we're sure. What a marriage this will be!

We tell everyone how perfectly matched we are. "We think alike about *everything!*" we rave. "We have the same standards, beliefs and values."

"Well, there are going to be problems," people might warn. To which we say quite happily, "Oh, sure! Of course there will be problems. We know *that!* But we're so good at communicating we'll work them out. You'll see."

Underscoring the confidence in our relationship skills is the knowledge that we're *In Love*. Love conquers all, everybody knows that. Problems? Piece of cake!

And it's true that with love all problems can be solved. Actually, they can be solved even *without* love, when there is enough communication and mutual respect.

But one of the biggest potential problems is often built into the marriage from the start. Most of us enter into marriage with an unspoken "contract," so to speak, and most of us assume that our spouse-to-be has the same contract in his or her mind.

The contract most of us have in mind reads something like this:

CONTRACT

1. I hereby agree to give you all the power in my life.

2. I renounce the right to make myself happy, knowing that from now on you will do it for me.

3. I will look to *you* for all my companionship, instead of having additional friends in my life.

4. Every need I now have, I expect you to fill.

5. In exchange, I will try to fill *your* every need. This gives me the right to advise and control you, because I know what is best for you.

6. With our responsibility for each other, we must match each other's moods. If you are angry, I will be angry, too. I'll be sad when you are sad, and expect sadness when I am sad. If one of us worries, the other must also worry. One must never be happy unless both are happy, no matter how long it takes . . . if ever.

7. Because you are the most important person in my life, should I ever be unhappy, it will clearly be your fault; and it is therefore your responsibility to try to reverse my mood.

8. Our signatures on this contract negate any responsibility for our individual selves that we might previously have held.

Signed:_____ and _____

There you have it, and I'm reasonably sure none of us would have signed it had it been presented to us before the wedding. And yet, foolish as those statements are, many of us expected marriage to "make us happy."

Notice that in most of the statements, one gives up responsibility and hands it over to one's mate. Granted, that would be a wonderful luxury, if it worked. Think how glorious it would be to have someone whose purpose in life is to make you happy, whatever that might take!

A fringe benefit would be the permission to blame all one's troubles on one's mate. "If I'm married and I'm unhappy I must have an unhappy marriage, and it's *your* fault. You're supposed to make me happy. It says so in the contract we signed."

You'll never hear anyone say those words because they sound so obviously unfair, and yet many of us unconsciously hold beliefs like those.

The first statement in the contract, "I hereby agree to give you all the power in my life," is clearly unthinkable. Oh, sometimes it can be a handy cop-out: "Gee, I'd love to come to your Tupperware party, but my husband won't let me go out at night."

But if the husband really *won't* let the wife go out at night, I would predict trouble down the road for that couple. When one person rules another, it is not a mutually respectful relationship, and the submissive one is almost sure to rebel somewhere along the way.

One possible exception is a traditional religious marriage, in which wives willingly agree to let their husbands make the rules. I do know some very happy couples who subscribe to that decision, but it works only when both people keep their part of the bargain. I'll address that issue in a later chapter.

Most of us are comfortable living in relationships based

on equality. But admittedly that takes enormous amounts of decision making and discussion of needs and wants. We may *want* equal rights and equal responsibility, but be unwilling to spend the time it takes to work out such an arrangement.

But you can't have it both ways. If you want to share the load equally you must accept the idea of continuing conversation, compromise, negotiation and respectful communication for the life of the marriage.

On the other hand, if you want to have all the power, you have to take responsibility for "making your partner happy." If you want to be the one without responsibility, you need to give up your autonomy and learn to enjoy the freedom that comes from making no decisions. It's all a trade-off.

If you did choose to give your mate all the power in your life (although I certainly don't recommend it), you could then state the second belief on the contract: "I renounce the right to make myself happy, knowing that from now on you will do it for me."

I know men and women who seem to have that expectation. They appear to be totally lost if the other person gets involved in activities that exclude them. It's as if marriage became their only source of happiness and their mate the only provider of it. Ooh, what a horrible concept! I shudder to think how miserable I'd be if *all* my happiness depended on Larry; or his on me. Thank God for all the opportunities we have to make *ourselves* happy, whether married or unmarried. We can make ourselves happy at any given hour of the day or night.

Granted, sometimes it's a challenge. If I've got stomach flu and am throwing up at 2:00 in the morning, it's nearly impossible to make myself happy! But it's just as impossible for Larry to make me happy in those circumstances. Meanwhile, I can always choose a nice book to read while I rest between trips to the bathroom.

But many of us complain profusely about this part of the contract. I admit I've done it a million times myself: "Larry loves sports so much he's never there to do things with me." Sniff. Even so, I'm confident that if we were asked to agree to this statement before the wedding, we would probably decline the offer.

"Whitney, will you marry me?"

"Sure, Jason. As long as I no longer have to make myself happy. You *will* do it for me, won't you?"

The sad thing is Jason might even agree. And both he and Whitney will believe it! That is the price of being in love; we think we can do anything.

Actually I've found people to be quite consistently happy or unhappy regardless of whether they're married or single. People either know how to enjoy life or they don't. Getting married doesn't alter that fact. Getting old doesn't either. Old, young, married or single, we decide to make ourselves happy—or unhappy. One thing I know for sure: No one else can do it for us.

I have heard, however, people blame their problems entirely on their mates. Mothers of unhappy adults sometimes say, "You know, Kathy was happy when she lived at home with her family. She was always laughing and carefree until she married Phil. He's got to be the cause of her problems."

Though that might seem to make sense, it's more likely that Kathy was happy at home because her family spoiled her. Parents who try to make their children's lives completely happy might be depriving them of the opportunity to grow and develop self-reliance. Regardless of whom those children marry, they may never be able to find a mate who treats them as dotingly as good old Mom or Dad did.

It may be that Kathy will leave Phil only to find that nobody else "makes her happy," either. She needs to develop her own resources if she is ever to be happy—or else live the rest of her life with Mom and Dad to nurture her.

In any case, I wouldn't agree to that part of the contract if I were you. God forbid you should ever find yourself entirely responsible for someone else's happiness!

Let's go on to the third statement, "I will look to *you* for all my companionship, instead of having additional friends in my life."

More women than men seem to make this mistake, although I see both sexes do it. We *should* be each other's best friend when we marry, but never each other's *only* friend.

For one thing, we can't think like the members of the opposite sex. Hard as I try, I can't imagine what goes on in men's minds. Obviously, they can't comprehend my thoughts and feelings, either, or we wouldn't have the misunderstandings we do. Men understand other men easily, just as women understand other women. Remember Professor Higgins in *My Fair Lady* singing, "Why can't a woman be more like a man?"

Listen to a group of women at a party commiserating about men. You'll generally hear at least one say, "I can't believe he didn't know how I felt." I can. Men rarely know quite how women feel. But all the women will nod with understanding and share their stories of disappointment in men's behavior.

Now listen to a group of men at the same party. Will their conversation be the same? No way. They'll be talking about sports, politics or their jobs. We women *wish* they'd be discussing us, but in truth they're tickled to death to have people around them who don't even *want* to talk about feelings and relationships.

So we need friends of our own sex. Each of my women friends fills a different role in my life. With some I talk about our kids and our houses. Some always like discussing men. A few like to dig into things like feminism or politics. Some are soft, others tougher. Some are genuinely interested in what I have to say. Others talk nonstop, but are very entertaining. Although I treasure them all, I'd hate to be on a desert island with only one friend.

Now *I* happen to believe that we should have friends of the opposite sex as well, but a lot of folks disagree with me. I maintain we can stay faithful to a mate and still enjoy other men and women as friends.

Unfortunately the number of extramarital affairs around us does tend to lend credibility to those who say, "No we can't. Look at him and her and her and him; all cheating on their spouses."

I can't deny it happens. But not with me. And not with the vast number of people who make the decision to stay faithful and do exactly that. If I ever cheated I'd have to eat my words, admit I erred and give up my men friends. That thought alone will keep me faithful!

I say anyone can stay faithful and still enjoy friends of the opposite sex. I must emphasize, however, that openness and honesty are essential when we have friends of both sexes. I have to be able to say, "Frank and I had lunch" as naturally and openly as I say, "Virginia and I had lunch." The minute I start withholding the fact that I'm having lunch with Frank is the minute I'm heading for trouble.

So? Cancel out number three in the contract. I'll look to others for companionship as well as to you, my dear husband. Aren't you glad?

What about statement number four, "Every need I now have I expect you to fill." Dumb, huh? But I know women who pumped their own gas when they were single and now expect their men to do it for them. "It's a man's job to take care of cars. Why haven't you changed my oil?"

There is certainly nothing wrong with a division of labor. If a man doesn't mind taking over the car care and a woman doesn't mind taking over the laundry, that is great. That is simply cooperation. (If they both want to keep up their survival skills they could trade every three months.) But when dependency rears its ugly head and men "can't" cook and women "can't" pull up weeds or do income-tax forms, they both lose something.

It's better to say, "Every need I have that I can possibly fill, I'll continue to fill. I'd appreciate it if you will do the same. But I'm also open to negotiation and sharing certain responsibilities."

The corollary to that is statement number five, "In exchange I will try to fill *your* every need. This gives me the right to advise and control you, because I know what is best for you."

This trap is awfully easy to fall into, especially for women. We tend to be good caretakers and nurturers, and in acting out of love we become motherly to our husbands if we're not careful. To fix a sumptuous dinner is a loving thing to do. But insisting he eat the vegetables is overstepping.

Women have an amazing ability to notice people's needs and wishes. A woman at the dinner table usually sees when someone is looking for the salt and provides it right away. But that same trait can mean that a woman notices *everything* and becomes a sort of guardian.

"Honey, I don't think you should wear that jacket; it's

too big," I told Larry one night.

"I love this jacket," he said contentedly, and left the house wearing it proudly.

I bit my tongue and disapproved.

Next time he put it on I managed a loving smile and a sugary voice as I said, "Sweetie, that jacket is so big it makes you look awful."

He gave me a quick kiss, smiled and zipped up the jacket.

Each time he wore it I would roll my eyes, giggle or make snide remarks. Even as I did it I knew it wasn't my business. Maybe it was all right the first time I mentioned it. But when he assured me he liked the jacket anyway, I should have accepted that. What makes me think I know best? I don't know, but I confess I sure do think that a lot of the time.

I can give Larry good advice about everything from what to eat to how to do his job. There is nothing I don't know! And I'll delightedly share it even if he doesn't want the benefit of my wisdom. In case he didn't hear me the first time (or the thirty-first), I'll repeat it in different ways. I might even mention it to the kids, hoping they'll mention it to him.

In my defense (of which there is precious little), I think that bad habit has its roots in loving and caring. "I love you so much I'll help you every way I can. Now, do things the way I tell you. It's for your own good, of course. Whatever would you do without me?"

This habit can drive people to drink. It isn't reserved only for women; some men do it, too. Often these people are excellent executives or workers who have a great deal of control over others. They *think* that way: "What does this company need to increase efficiency?" And then they go home and give instructions to dust first and vacuum second rather than the other way around. Huge arguments result! "Look, I'm only trying to make your job easier. Vacuuming first doesn't get the dust you brush onto the floor when you dust first. Don't you *see?*" (I actually had a couple in counseling who belabored that point for half a session.)

The point is, it doesn't matter. My friend George says, "It's practically impossible to overestimate the unimportance of almost anything."

He's right. Let's show our love by letting people decide for themselves what to wear, what to eat, how to clean, etc., etc. It's so much more respectful than believing they need our advice.

The next point in the contract addresses feelings and behavior based on emotions. It's surprising how suggestible we are to other people's moods. Let one bummed-out person be grim and grouchy long enough and hard enough, and the entire family/office/classroom may very well follow suit. It seems almost contagious to have someone around exhibiting strong feelings. If that's true in a work setting, it's even more valid at home.

We almost seem to *believe,* "With our responsibility for each other we must match each others' moods."

Perhaps it seems like showing respect for another's crankiness to act cranky, too. I am aware of a certain reluctance to sing and dance for joy in the same room where someone is acting darkly angry. But isn't it foolish? I wonder why we feel we must tiptoe around a person who is at odds with his world. Maybe we're afraid of appearing unsympathetic.

But at least it's something we can ponder and discuss with those we care about. We could ask them if they *want* us to match their moods. I'm guessing most of them would say, "Of course not." Given that permission, then, would we be willing and able to act however we feel? Or would we continue to be quiet and withdrawn when our mates are? We can only try it and find out.

The agreement, "If you are angry I will be angry, too," may depend on who is the object of your anger. If you're angry at a co-worker or a neighbor, I'll be glad to join in and play *Ain't it awful?* with you. We can both badmouth the jerk and have a marvelous drama in which we agree (for once). It *is* fun to have a common enemy at times. We can give it our all for ten minutes and then put it aside and do something fun.

But if it's *me* with whom you're angry, that is a horse of another color. No way will I join you in being angry at *me!* Instead, I'll probably get very angry at you for being angry at me. And we can play out that scene for a lot longer than ten minutes. How about all evening? Maybe even all week. You want anger, you got it, Buster.

See, I have to do that in order to punish you for your anger. My private logic says that if I punish you enough, you'll start acting like I want you to act; loving me dearly at all times and never getting upset with me. Most of us are pros at manipulating people with our emotions.

My friend and colleague John Daley maintains that any time we're angry for longer than ten minutes we're trying to manipulate a person or a situation.

When I first heard him say that I was dubious. But I've checked it out many times and now agree with him. If I bump my head on a cupboard door I may feel a surge of anger for . . . what, maybe a minute or two? Not for long, because there is no one to manipulate. I won't stay mad at a cupboard door, and I certainly don't want to stay mad at myself. So I quit being angry.

But let *you* do or say something that hurts me and I can stay angry at you for a long, long time. I probably won't even have the awareness that I'm trying to "whip you into shape" by making you uncomfortable.

Anger does beget anger. We'll talk more about that later. All we need to do now is decide whether or not we choose to continue being angry just because someone else is.

The same is true for the remaining statements, too, about matching sadness with sadness and worry with worry, and not being happy until the other one is. It's all part of the unconscious belief that we should feel the same at all times.

Though it may be difficult *not* to get dragged down when another person is, we can give ourselves and each other permission to work at improving the ability. Will the upset person think we're unsympathetic? Possibly, if they've been used to getting sympathy in the form of a glum face that matches their own. But once we establish our insight and motives, those around us can begin getting used to this new, better way to live.

Remember the old song, "I can be happy; I can be sad; I can be good; I can be bad; it all depends on you!"

What a hell-on-earth existence that would be, and yet many of us allow ourselves to wind up in that situation. We need to see that we've put ourselves there, recognize how foolish it is and quit doing it.

The next statement in the contract says, "Because you are the most important person in my life, should I ever be unhappy it will clearly be your fault; and it is, therefore, your responsibility to try to reverse my mood."

Notice that word "try."

Did you every try to make happy someone who is determined to stay unhappy? Most of us have. Most of us have been in the opposite position, too, fiercely hanging onto our unhappiness while someone tries to cheer us up.

There is almost a triumphant ecstacy in staying miserable just to defeat them!

The song continues, "I can save money; or spend it; go right on living; or end it; you're to blame, honey; for what I do."

How marvelous to be able to blame you for all my behavior! We all enjoy having someone to blame. In fact, I have a good friend named Eric who volunteers to be this someone. He's got an unparalleled sense of humor and is virtually unflappable, and he says, "Hey, if you want anyone to blame for your problems you can blame me. I don't care." So I hereby invite you to blame all your woes on good old Eric. He can stand it!

We won't do that, of course, because that would end the game playing we so enjoy with our mates. If I'm angry at Larry for inviting an unexpected dinner guest, I don't want to blame Eric. Nor do I want to forget the incident. I certainly don't want to forgive Larry or he might do it again.

No, I have only one course of action: Blame him long enough and hard enough so he will never again even *consider* doing anything like that. I've got to teach him a lesson he won't soon forget.

Now, of course, I wouldn't deliberately and consciously think those thoughts, because that would make me a mean, controlling, self-centered shrew. I won't disclose my feelings or my goals. I'll just be cool and withdrawn. Larry will figure it all out sooner or later.

Of course, if I really want to solve the issue in a respectful way I might say something like this: "Honey, when you bring home an unexpected guest for dinner I feel really embarrassed because I look like death and also because all we have in the house is that Eggplant Surprise that nobody would eat. I need your help to find a solution."

That opens the way for respectful negotiation, which is far more likely to solve the problem.

Well, that about wraps up the contract. It *is* tempting to sign something that promises, "Our signatures negate any responsibility for our individual selves that we might previously have held." Zowie! Freedom from responsibility! What a heady thought.

It reminds me of the time in third grade when Sister Mary Domitilla told the class that if any of us ever gave someone else permission to sin, we would have that sin on *our* souls. The class Rotten Kid named Jimmy raised his hand and asked, "Sister, if somebody tells me I can do something bad, then does that mean I get off scot-free?"

Sister assured him firmly that it meant *both* people would be guilty of the same sin.

Well, heck. If giving somebody else the responsibility for my life isn't going to get me off scot-free, then maybe I won't sign the contract. Not just yet, anyway. Let's finish the book and think about it.

Chapter 4

Male and Female

One of the first questions I intend to ask God when I get to heaven is why he made women and men so different. The longer I live the more amazed I am that the sexes manage to get along at all! We deserve medals.

It's no wonder both sexes are fraught with disappointment and frustration. We think that because we're all human beings there must be some similarity in our thought processes. In truth we might do just as well trying to communicate with creatures from other planets.

Men and women don't think alike, let alone speak the same language. Our needs are vastly different, as are our expectations.

When we say the words, "I do," we're foolish enough to believe we're both agreeing to the same principles. Maybe those words should be changed to "I wish" or "I want." Or "I will if you will." We should stick in a bunch of "unlesses" and "except whens."

But if we rewrote the marriage ceremony, defining attitudes, expectations and gender differences, we'd have 300 pages with lots of "whereas . . ." phrases. It would be a hopelessly complicated legal process that would stop any of us from attempting it.

So it's just as well we stick with the simplistic format we have, because it allows us in our naiveté to enter marriage with confidence, false though it may be.

All we really need to change is our belief system—that men and women are reasonably alike. Instead, we have to accept the truth—that the rare occasions on which we see things with the same perspective are only happy accidents.

For one thing, women tend to think in great detail. We grasp millions of trivialities in any one experience, engrave them indelibly on our photographic memories and assume men do the same thing. Men, on the other hand, think way more broadly, in global terms, dismissing the trivialities as unimportant.

Why do we entertain the idea, then, that a couple can easily communicate with pleasure for any great length of time?

Here is a couple going home from a dinner party.

She: Carolyn is the best cook in town. The way she heated the brie just ever so slightly and then topped it with a sauce that was sweet but with some horseradish to make it zingy! Wasn't that good?!

He: Good food!

She: She does everything like that. She must have had a million classes in gourmet cooking. There was mint in the vegetables, too. I noticed that their friends from Nevada were pretty miffed with each other, did you?

He: Who?

She: The couple from Nevada.

He: Who were they?

She: They sat right across from us. She was wearing a turquoise cotton top and a white skirt and lots of Indian jewelry; and he had on a denim shirt and Levis. Did you notice his watch? Indian made. It had the biggest obsidian stones I've ever seen. It was magnificent, wasn't it?

He: Oh, the guy who used to be a Marine?

She: I don't know what he *did*. I just could see that he and his wife were hostile. Did you notice how she never laughed at his jokes?

He: He was a Marine. He was telling us about the war. Fascinating stuff.

She: But I wonder why they were so mad at each other. When everyone clinked glasses during the toast they avoided each other's.

He: We talked politics. He's a strong Republican.

She: He sure drinks a lot. He had three scotch and sodas before dinner, about five glasses of wine during dinner and two brandies after.

He: (silent)

She: Did you notice?

He: Notice what?

She: How much he drank. I thought he'd fall asleep at the table, he looked so snockered.

He: (long silence)

She: So, what else did you guys talk about?

He: Oh, I don't know . . . the World Series . . . Iran . . . the greenhouse effect.

Somehow the conversation doesn't seem to jibe. And when they're en route to another dinner party six months later it will go like this.

She: I wonder if the Nevada couple will be there again tonight.

He: Who?

She: The couple from Nevada, remember? She wore the turquoise cotton top and all the Indian jewelry; he wore denim and Levis and a watch with big obsidian stones; and they were hostile. Remember? They avoided each other all evening; didn't even clink glasses during the toast; she never laughed at his jokes; and he was a Marine, you said.

He: Hmm. I do remember an ex-Marine, I think. I'm sure looking forward to watching the game after dinner.

And we wonder why they have problems in so many areas. The way they perceive life touches every facet of their marriage. Like birthdays. She will remember that he likes smoked almonds, and she'll buy him some and present them elegantly wrapped, along with a shirt of a color he doesn't have, two ties that accent it perfectly, monogrammed stationery and his favorite aftershave.

Furthermore, she will have *enjoyed* the process of shopping for just the right card, wrapping each gift in different paper, and fixing a sumptuous dinner with a birthday cake and candles. She's good at all of those things.

The catch is, she expects her birthday to be remembered with the same care and thoughtfulness.

I can't tell you how many tearful wives I see within a week after their birthdays.

"My birthday was Wednesday. I thought for sure he'd buy me *one* of the things I'd said I wanted. I talked about at least ten things I wanted in the worst way. He could have bought any of them, and I would have been thrilled. But no, he did nothing about it. I waited all day. I thought maybe I'd get flowers delivered—I had balloons sent to his office for his birthday. But no . . . no flowers, no card. That night I hardly spoke to him. He finally realized. He raced out and bought flowers and a card at the supermarket and said I should go pick out something special as a gift from him the next day. Well, let me tell you, I didn't, and I won't. I can't believe how insensitive he was. And after all I did for him on his birthday!"

It's basically a difference in the sexes. He flat doesn't remember details. But he can be trained to, if he realizes the importance of it.

I recommend that wives begin talking about it a month before their birthday. Put up a wish list on the refrigerator and talk about it often, adding gifts you'd like from time to time. Define the perfect birthday. Tell him where you'd like to eat out, if you want him to get a sitter, if you want to include the kids in the celebration, etc., etc.

"But that takes all the fun out of it," wives protest. "I want *him* to think of it! I want spontaneity and surprise!"

"You can have all that someday," I reassure them, "but you have to do the training now. In just a few years he'll know what to expect, and you won't be so disappointed."

Children need to be taught how to dust furniture, how to wash dishes, how to do things the way we want them done. Employees in new jobs require training, and employers *expect* to teach. People of all ages take classes to learn skills they didn't previously have.

So it is with a relationship, only we rarely stop and think about it. We expect each other to think and act the same as we do. All we need is the open-mindedness to teach each other what we'd like.

It's hard, though, for men to *act* the way women want them to because they don't *feel* the way women want them to. They can't. There are innate differences in men and women besides the obvious physical ones.

One doctor explained it to a women's group I attended. He said, "Little boy and little girl babies are identical at first. At conception they're both little girls. But early on in the pregnancy the boys get a big bath of testosterone and that changes them dramatically. In fact," he twinkled, "it destroys a part of their brain, the part that thinks and feels like little girls think and feel."

The women all tittered, of course, and reveled in the thought that "we're dealing with brain-damaged people here. That explains a lot!"

I think the good doctor was an expert at wrapping the audience around his finger, but I suspect what he was getting at was the true physical differences in the brains of men and women.

You can't get a cow to think like a lion. I believe women are more disappointed in men than vice versa, because women's minds expect a lot more attention to detail than is comfortable for men's minds.

Women seem able to think of six different things at the same time. A woman can carry on a phone conversation while she chops celery for the soup, fixes peanut-butter sandwiches for the kids and motions them in to eat while she's letting in the paperboy and getting out the checkbook, writing him a check, wiping the kids' faces and sending them off to play . . . all the time planning what to fix for dinner.

If a man is on the phone and his wife whispers loudly, "Tell Jack we'll bring back the hedge trimmer tomorrow," the man usually looks confused, shakes his head to indicate he doesn't understand and continues talking. She repeats the message, uses body language to demonstrate hedge trimmers and says loudly, "We'll return it tomorrow," but he continues looking totally blank. Finally he says with some annoyance, "Just a minute, Jack," sets down the phone and asks, "What *is* it?" Only then can he comprehend the message.

I know that is not true of every man, and to you men out there who are bristling at unfair generalizations, I apologize. I know better than to believe all generalizations, and I realize there are many men who can run circles around women when it comes to carrying on six different thought processes at the same time.

I recognize, too, that women may be accusing me of old, sexist stereotyping. They're thinking, "She's got us chopping celery and doing kitchen things like women did in the forties. Doesn't she know there are women like me who are CEOs? I'm president of a corporation. I do things besides wipe peanut butter off my kids' faces!"

Yes, and I'll bet those chief executives are doing six things at once from their polished oak desks in their penthouse offices overlooking the city. They can apply their detail ability to whatever setting they are in.

But my point is this: Women think along several tracks at the same time. Men focus on one or two until they finish, then turn their attention to one or two more. That can be a plus. They're putting a more concerted effort on one task, spending the major part of their energy on solving that one problem before they attack another. They are often less fragmented than women, and more goal oriented. Often their endurance level is far superior to women's.

When I see TV clips of men working to put out forest fires, for example, I'm mightily impressed with their tenacity. They appear before the cameras looking exhausted, unshaven, discouraged, but relentless in their battle and dedicated to their goal. The same with rescue teams, for a mine tragedy or a missing child. Men go willingly to meet the need and continue unceasingly until the job is done. Everything in them is focused on that one need. I'm glad they have that ability because *I* certainly don't.

I like men's strength. I admire their selfless tenacity and dedication to doing a job well. But I want them to think more like women, to be more conversational, more into feelings.

I don't think we can have it both ways. But that doesn't stop us from wishing we could. That is where the pain comes from: Our expectations are disappointed too often.

Lisa said one day, "Maybe we're looking to men for something they don't have to give. It's like picking up a dog and trying to iron with it. You'd say, 'Darn it, this dog isn't getting the wrinkles out.' You can't blame the dog for not being an iron." Sounds sensible to me.

Maybe we need to be more appreciative of the qualities that make men different from us rather than wishing they were more *like* us. Ideally we would complement each other, each having strengths the other lacks.

Men can make terrific playmates! Most men are eager participants in anything that smacks of fun, and we women don't take enough advantage of that. They're always delighted with an adventure, whether it's a game in which they compete or one where they watch others compete. They'll even indulge in a food fight if you will. They have so much "little boy" still inside them that they can help us be more childlike and open to playing, if we let them.

Usually we won't. We're so busy being sensible that we don't have time to play. Women always "need to talk." We're a pretty serious lot, we women, wanting to straighten out all our problems "if it takes all night."

I think it's good that at least one of us will be a driving force to keep communication going, but we should have fun as well.

Interestingly, much of the playing children do is already indicative of the differences in sexes. The very sounds they make, for instance, as they're learning to talk. There was a study that showed baby boys make noises most of the time when they're experimenting with talking. Meaningless noises, but in great variety. Baby girls try to say words and string them together in sentences even before they can actually talk.

Our grandson Christopher began shooting with imaginary guns when he was barely two and didn't even own a toy gun. He would break off part of a cracker and aim at trees and make shooting sounds.

At the same age, the little girl across the street was lovingly holding her baby doll.

In addition to the innate sexual differences, of course, men and women are separated by the roles that have been taught us for hundreds of years. It's very difficult to change the pictures in our minds that define "how men act" and "what women do."

One of the major differences is how we deal with anger. Men are generally comfortable expressing their feelings in a confrontive way. In a work setting, a man can release anger audibly and forcefully to his employees and/or colleagues, and he's respected for his aggressiveness.

Women, on the other hand, are called "bitchy" if they have the audacity to be as vehemently vocal.

Dr. Harriet Goldhor Lerner described it very well in her book, *The Dance of Anger.*[1] I quote her:

"Women have long been discouraged from the awareness and forthright expression of anger. Sugar and spice are the ingredients from which we are made. We are the nurturers, the soothers, the peacemakers and the steadiers of rocked boats. It is our job to please, protect and placate the world. We may hold relationships in place as if our lives depended on it.

"Women who openly express anger at men are especially suspect. Even when society is sympathetic to our goals of equality, we all know that 'those angry women' turn everybody off. Unlike our male heroes, who fight and

even die for what they believe in, women may be con-
demned for waging a bloodless and humane revolution
for their own rights. The direct expression of anger, especially at men, makes us unladylike, unfeminine, unmater-
nal, sexually unattractive or, more recently, 'strident.'
Even our language condemns such women as 'shrews,'
'witches,' 'bitches,' 'hags,' 'nags,' 'man-haters' and 'castra-
tors.' They are unloving and unlovable. They are devoid
of femininity. Certainly you do not wish to become one
of *them*. It is an interesting sidelight that our language—
created and codified by men—does not have *one* unflat-
tering term to describe men who vent their anger at
women. Even such epithets as 'bastard' and 'son of a bitch'
do not condemn the man, but place the blame on a
woman—his mother!"

Dr. Lerner's book is one of my favorites and I often recommend it to men *and* women.

It's difficult to know just how much of our difference
in attitude and behavior is innate and physiological, and
how much is unconsciously learned from role models we
observed. The line that separates the two will no doubt
always be fuzzy, but we can agree that the sexes act and
think and feel very differently from one another.

Some of the differences will diminish as society gets
better at equality. Some never will, though, because we're
not "created equal" in the womb.

And that is good.

When it comes right down to it, we seem not to want
to be married to people who are exactly like us. I know
a few men who think more like I do than Larry does. But
the attraction is not there for me. Men to whom I gravitate
have different personalities from mine.

When our daughter Laurie married Pete, their friends
described it as "James Dean and Doris Day," so opposite

were they. But they seem to be good for each other in creating a balance. Their son Christopher is lucky to have two vastly different people to watch and learn from. Undoubtedly he'll pick up traits from each, but basically he'll always be *male*. He'll never be able (or want) to think and feel like a female, even though his wife will probably wish he would.

It's only a matter of time until he puts aside his guns made out of crackers and marries the little girl across the street. She will assume, of course, that he feels exactly like he does about her baby dolls and everything else that is important to her. It will take them both a while to discover how differently they feel about almost everything.

1. Dr. Harriet Goldhor Lerner, *The Dance of Anger,* New York, Perennial Library, 1985.

Chapter 5

The Secret Skill

Any of you who are parents and any of you who *had* parents know that parents teach their children many skills that will help them be happy, fit in and be successful in society.

Most skills are taught and labeled very clearly. "Christopher, this is how you dig with a shovel. See? Take the shovel like this, put the dirt here. Now you can stick this little plant in the hole. Let's water it and watch it grow. That's how you garden. Christopher is going to be a good little gardener!"

"Christopher, our friends are coming over for brunch today. When they hold out their hands, like this, you shake hands with them, like this. Give them a nice smile and say 'How do you do?'"

"Ah-h-h-k, Christopher, no no no! Don't unroll the whole roll of foil!"

"I *liked* the way you hung up your jammies, Christopher. It's good to be neat."

That's called *parenting*.

Every child ever born got more parenting than he or she would have liked, and learned vast amounts of useful information before ever starting school, finding the process never ending. Parents love to teach their children.

But there is one social skill we parents teach without ever mentioning it. We would never ever give it a name. It must be done subtly. Still, even though we don't define it, we teach it more certainly than we teach gardening techniques. We model it daily, sometimes even constantly.

By the time the child is five he's almost as good at it as his parents. He understands it, can do it himself, knows when other people are doing it and how he should respond, but he hasn't the foggiest idea of its name.

He may hear it defined for the first time in his twenties or thirties and suddenly realize that he can do that! Or, more likely, he realizes that someone around him does that. Over the years he becomes more aware of the universality of the skill. In his forties and fifties he's incredulous at its continued use and proven power.

What is this skill?

Manipulation.

It permeates the atmosphere, affecting every relationship. Not only do mothers and fathers use it, so do children, teachers, lovers, executives and workers in every capacity. It's like the air around us, ever-present, and we take it for granted as we do air. It's what *is*.

Among Webster's definitions of manipulation are these: "To treat or manage with the intellect. To control the action of, by management; to manage artfully or fraudulently."

Gracious. It sounds like we wouldn't want to teach *that* to our children anymore than we would lying, stealing or cheating. But teach it we do, expertly, thoroughly, unceasingly . . . and in exactly the same ways our parents taught it to us: by giving frequent demonstrations. We may even have fine-tuned the manipulative skills we learned from our parents, and refined them into a masterful art that we hand down to our babies as soon as possible.

Why do we do that? Because manipulation works! Whatever works is something we want to use and keep and polish. We only get rid of something if it *doesn't* work. Manipulation is so effective that it will probably be kept in our families for generations, maybe forever.

Are there any better ways to get our needs met? Of course there are, but am I willing to give up the old tried-and-true skill of manipulation? Gee, I doubt it. I've used it for so long that I'm afraid I'd miss it if it weren't around.

Imagine the scene if manipulation *were* taught like other lessons are taught. Mother might pick up her toddler, hug and kiss her and say, "Baby, today I'm going to teach you something wonderful! You're going to love it. It's something you can do whenever there is something you want and it looks like you're not going to get it. It's called 'manipulation.' Can you say that word?"

"Ma-nip-a-shun?" Baby lisps.

"Very good! Now this is what it means. Say you want a new doll at the toy store in the mall. You ask Daddy for it and he says no. You really want that doll, so you coax him a little. But he still says you can't have it. Now here comes the good part. You ma-nip-u-late Daddy. You look very, very sad and you walk slowly. Make sure you keep looking down at your feet. Don't say a word, now. Sooner or later Daddy will notice that you're looking at your feet, walking ever so slowly and not talking and he'll say, 'What's wrong, Baby?'

"Now I know you'll want to tell him, but you mustn't tell him yet. You sigh first. Can you sigh? Like this. Good!

Good girl! You make your voice very, very soft and you say kind of pitifully, 'Nothing, Daddy.'"

Baby: But something *is*. I want my doll.

Mommy: I know, dear, but you have to do it this way, because this way works. Trust Mommy. Mommy *knows*. You keep walking more and more slowly, looking sadder and sadder. Never ever look right at Daddy, you understand? Always look away from him. When you get to the car and he's fastening your seat belt, start to cry very quietly. He'll ask again what's wrong.

Baby: Can I tell him now?

Mommy: No, not yet. Be patient. Sometimes it takes a long time. You ask him for a hankie to wipe your eyes and you keep crying, looking sad and looking away from him. Now, it may not work right away, Baby. You may have to look sad and sigh a lot for a few more days before Daddy will go back and get you the doll. But don't look at him, whatever you do. Except at bedtime when he kisses you good night. Then look right into his eyes and say, "I love you, Daddy," and hug him very tight. Then turn away and sigh a big, loud sigh.

Baby: Like this? (sigh-h-h-h)

Mommy: Perfect! Oh, Baby, Mommy's so proud of you! You're going to be a good little manipulator like Mommy is! Now, you watch me a lot and you'll see more and more how easy it is to do. In fact tonight at dinner I'm going to ask Daddy to paint the kitchen. Watch carefully and see Mommy manipulate!

End of lesson. And I can imagine you male readers feeling a kind of vengeful, "A-ha! I *knew* it was a carefully thought-out system." But men, too, are masters of the art. Let's peek at another scenario.

Dad: C'mon, sport, Dad's gonna teach you a new game.

Sport: Oh, boy, like soccer?

Dad: No, this one doesn't take a ball or anything like that. This is a game that helps you get whatever you want.

Sport: *Anything,* Daddy?

Dad: Anything, sport. And it helps you get out of doing things you don't want to do, too. Let's say Mom wants you to clean your room and you don't want to. You can't just refuse; you'd get in trouble. You learn to manipulate.

Sport: Oh, boy!

Dad: See, women can't stand it when men get mad at them. That's your best bet when you don't want to do something, get mad at them. First you put it off as long as you can; that's called *procrastinating.* But when you finally have to buckle down and clean the room, make sure you look real mad. Throw things around in there. Slam a couple of drawers. You can even say some bad words if you want. When you're done—and by the way, don't do a good job; that's *real* important—come out looking like a thundercloud, you know what I mean?

Sport: You mean like you looked when Mom asked you to transplant the rosebush? Is that like a thundercloud?

Dad: Right on, sport. You got it! Ha, ha, you're gonna be a great thundercloud, kid. You're my kid! And don't speak to her. If you have to say anything at all, glare at her. Before long she'll quit asking you to do anything. She'll do it herself because she won't want to see you glaring at her.

Sport: How long do I have to glare and not speak to her, Dad?

Dad: Ah, good question, sport! Keep it up all day for sure, and maybe even the next day or two. Except if you're talking to someone else. Say if your buddy comes over, it's okay to talk and laugh and have fun. Just act like Mom isn't even there. But when he leaves, make sure you get real quiet again. Someday when you have a wife you'll have this thing down to a science. It's how men have to treat women. I used to see my dad do that to my mom. Just act mad and quit talking when they bug you about *anything*. Eventually they quit bugging. Now, keep your eye out and watch me the next time she asks me to do something.

Let's go on to the scene when Mommy asks Daddy to paint the kitchen. Both children's eyes are wide as they watch the drama unfold.

Mom: Honey, how about another cup of coffee? I got the mandarin-chocolate blend you like so much and ground the beans myself. Was it a good day? You certainly looked nice this morning when you left. I was proud of you. You look so much younger than our friends' husbands.

Dad: Yeah? Thanks! (grins broadly) Sure, I'll have another cup. It's great.

Mom: I've been wanting to have your boss and his wife over for dinner.

Dad: That would be fine. Say when and I'll mention it to him.

Mom: The only thing that's holding me back is how awful this kitchen looks.

Dad: Looks fine to me. What's wrong with it?

Mom: Oh, honey, it's terrible! It's needed painting for two years now.

Dad: Yeah, well, it's not bad, really.

Mom: Not bad! I couldn't possibly have people in when the house looks like *this*. Especially your boss.

Dad: Then don't have them. Or don't let 'em in the kitchen. (laughs) Hey, it's time for *Cheers*.

Mom: But, honey, let's decide about the kitchen.

Dad: What's to decide? I don't have time to paint, if

that's what you mean.

Mom: Sigh-h-h-h. (Baby's eyes widen with interest.) I just want to help you have the kind of image that will impress your boss. I try so *hard* to help you. Maybe I can paint it myself. (Sigh-h-h.) I could get up early in the mornings, like at four o'clock or so, so I could get in a couple hours of painting before I iron your shirts and buy groceries for you to eat.

Dad: For *me* to eat? Don't *you* eat? Can't I have any peace around here, for God's sake? It's nag, nag, nag the minute I come through the door. You think I don't work hard enough all day that I feel like coming home and working hard here, too? You don't want a husband. You want a slave you can boss around!

Dad exits angrily and turns on the TV while Sport watches eagerly.

Mom cleans up the kitchen quietly, blowing her nose from time to time. Later she joins the family in the living room and talks to the children, but avoids looking at Dad. The children have just seen the lesson of manipulation acted out before their very eyes.

To complete the demonstration, both parents continue modeling their prescribed behavior for days. They go about their roles with practiced ease, playing their parts with magnificent timing and expertise.

Eventually Dad paints the kitchen, making sure to splash paint on almost every surface. He glares and glowers except when his buddy stops by and they take a few hours off to watch a game. He finishes the paint job in stony silence, icily ignoring any attempts Mom makes toward friendliness, and continues that behavior for an additional week.

Baby is learning that Mom's techniques did indeed get the kitchen painted. Sport observes how men operate in order to avoid being controlled. We can be sure that by the time they're ready to marry, they will have developed the same expertise and timing as Mom and Dad.

The problem with manipulation is, though, that while both partners are experts at their crafts, they won't necessarily be playing the same game.

When we try to manipulate each other, it's like I'm playing Monopoly and you're playing Chinese checkers. Both of us are playing our very best, and we're master players, but somehow it isn't working. We both *know* it isn't, and we're pretty sure the other person is playing "wrong." We try harder to make this game work, and we try to win, but it won't ever resolve because I'm using paper money and plastic houses while you're using marbles and dice.

We watch each other play and we feel increased frustration at the seeming hopelessness of the whole experience. *We* know the rules, but why doesn't the other person follow them?

The wife who says, "He should come ask me what's wrong when I'm crying in the bedroom," can't imagine herself failing to ask that of anyone crying anywhere.

The husband says, "The thing that turns me off more than anything else is when she cries. I refuse to get involved when she pulls that."

His game plan is: If I ignore her behavior long enough and hard enough she'll quit that crying nonsense.

Hers is: If I cry long enough and hard enough he's bound to feel sorry for me.

And there are 10,000 variations for every game. Those who grow up in the same family know all the rules and variations that were "taught" in their home, but even they are likely to have made different decisions on how to "beat the system."

This person never cries. He just sighs and looks sad. That one yells and screams. She quits speaking. He glowers. She gets drunk. He eats too much. She quits eating entirely. He develops a nervous stomach. These two cry constantly. Those two argue to win, but never to resolve an issue. He acts martyred. She has an affair. He tries to dominate and control. She goes limp and passive. He lies. She confronts. She denies. He accuses. She packs a suitcase and moves out. He romances.

And one of the funniest things is this: At some level, both people enjoy the whole process. Give it up? Change? Never!

I still remember the couple who yelled fiercely at each other, even shouting cruel obscenities, while I tried vainly to establish an atmosphere of order and respect in which we could work toward a sensible solution. After a few weeks the husband stopped cussing at the wife and turned to me. "Are you saying I shouldn't cuss at her?"

"Exactly what I'm saying," I beamed. "Just keep your voice at a respectful level and tell her what you want, how you feel, what you'd like from her."

"Let me ask you something," he said.

"Sure. What?"

"Don't you and your husband yell at each other?"

"No."

"Never?"

"Never."

"How the hell do you stand a boring relationship like that?" he demanded. He and his wife looked at each other in total agreement. A marriage without yelling and screaming was just too dull for them. They left together and never came back.

Changing our patterns of behavior is often an unacceptable option. We don't want to change. We just want the other guy to change. And probably the other guy doesn't want to change, either, even if he's uncomfortable.

Many of those who yell and scream rather like it. Who in his right mind, they wonder, would choose to give it up? The same is true for *any* kind of manipulative behavior. It's what we learned as children. We're experts at crying, pouting, rebelling, withdrawing or whatever we've practiced over the years. No way are we going to give it up.

But if we could let go of our unhealthy games, we would be amazed at the amount of time we'd have to enjoy. I often think of how simple life would be if we all agreed that on a certain date, everyone in the world would stop manipulating.

If we could get our needs and wants met without all the emotionalism we've been wasting, wouldn't it be terrific? To solve problems in a forthright, logical, respectful way without the tears and hurt and anger—is it possible?

You bet.

Then what's stopping us? Nothing.

Would that really improve our marriage? Magically!

So how do we start? Read on.

Chapter 6

Getting Our Needs
Met—The Right Way

First of all we must establish the fact that we have very few actual *needs*. Most of what we like to call *needs* are really *wants*. Certainly we prefer calling them *needs*, because that makes them seem essential to our very lives. We might be reluctant to ask for and expect someone to indulge us in whatever we *want*, but we have no such compunctions against expecting that treatment when our *needs* are concerned.

So our communication is peppered with the word. "I need sex every day," some husbands insist. To which I respond, "No, you don't. You might *want* sex every day, or five times a day, but you would survive very well without it." (They don't believe me.)

Probably our actual needs are only food, water and shelter. I'd throw in clothing and love, but I suspect we *could* survive without even those if we had to.

But life would be grim if all we ever had met were our needs. There is nothing wrong with wanting more, and we have every right to express our feelings, thoughts and descriptions of what we want out of life. We must simply recognize the difference between those wants and our needs.

Some common needs I hear expressed (or express myself) are these: I need at least nine hours of sleep. I need to have my coffee first thing in the morning. I need to know I'm appreciated. I need a lot of peace and quiet. I need privacy. I need people. I need excitement. I need security. I need constant change. I need affection.

I don't suppose people will ever change their conversational habits enough to use the word "need" only when it's absolutely true. But if we can recognize the word as slang and not allow ourselves to believe that our wants are needs, life may be a little less frustrating.

The quality of our lives depends a lot on what we want and how we attain it. We have the right to work for what we want as long as we're not hurting someone else in the process. Sometimes we have the right to work for what we want even if we *are* hurting someone else in the process. It's okay to punch out a thief who's robbing a little old lady, even if it's hurting the thief.

Young adults often enjoy chewing on moral concepts and discussing "truisms" that suddenly seem false to them, and that's good; that's growth. "Is it all right to steal a loaf of bread and give it to a starving child?" Hopefully even we "old" adults still enjoy pondering and discussing ethics and morality, and continuing to develop our beliefs.

All of that, however, explains why needs and wants become so confusing. I might genuinely believe I need something, or at least want it so strongly that I feel I must have it. Larry might believe exactly the opposite.

How in the world can two people with different wants survive together in harmony? Not easily, that's for sure. But certainly they have the capacity to resolve their differences in wants, and even to enjoy the process of resolution. Usually our mistakes lie in not expecting to have to deal with differences. Somehow we manage to convince ourselves that our wants make more sense than the other person's.

The "oughta wantas" rear their ugly heads, and we complain long and loudly about all the things our mates oughta wanta do, or like, or see, or avoid, or indulge in. "She oughta wanta have sex more often!" "He oughta wanta spend more time with me and the children!"

Our own wants are so strong that we can't imagine the other person's not being the same. We spend a tremendous amount of emotional energy trying to convince our partners that we're right and they're wrong.

Really, we could simplify our lives immeasurably by taking the right and wrong out of most discussions. Though some clear-cut behaviors are wrong to almost everybody, and other taboos are culturally or religiously or socially based. A great many are rooted only in our own unique thinking. ("This is right because I think it is, and you should think that way, too.")

So many fights are fought because of an innate "need" to win. To prove we're right and they're wrong. It's rare that we can change anybody's mind, but that doesn't stop us from trying.

The process of trying to change someone's mind is often actually fun, and I love to play the game with willing partners. My brother Paul and I can argue on any subject for hours on end without getting the least bit ruffled. It is a game in which no one has to give up anything or change in any way. Once in a while he'll convince me of something, and I suspect I've changed his thinking occasionally. But neither of us has an investment in the other one's changing.

That's a very different situation from trying to change our spouse's mind because his/her behavior is affecting our life! When we believe our happiness is being prevented by our mate's actions, we have a strong emotional investment in changing his or her mind. We play to win. We manipulate. We fight dirty. We go for the victory no matter what it costs. Often the issue is power: who's right?

A discouraged wife recounted a battle with her husband: "I am so jealous of his friend. My husband is like a kid with a best buddy, and they want to do everything together, like two little boys. Last night we had made plans to go to a movie together when the phone rang and it was his pal, Doug. I felt the hackles rise the minute I heard him say, 'Hey, buddy!' I knew Doug would be wanting him to do something, and I knew my husband would agree to it. I was making all these motions to him, shaking my head, begging him to decline, but sure enough, he agreed to go out with Doug. When he hung up I was furious at him, and guess what he said: 'If I had turned Doug down you would have *won*, and I would have resented losing to you.'"

Losing is threatening to most of us, and we often base our decisions on that one point.

In any relationship, we can have competition or cooperation, but never both at the same time. The only exception to that rule is playing in team sports, when we cooperate with our team and compete against the other team. But in marriage there is no team . . . just two individuals cooperating or competing.

When you compete, you can't possibly cooperate. And, of course, the best way to solve problems is through cooperation. When competition rears its ugly head in a love relationship it temporarily overrides the good feelings of tenderness and affection and revs up the fight-to-win mentality.

I did say "temporarily," however, and the minute we become aware of competition we can withdraw and change our direction.

Probably the simplest way to proceed would be with self-disclosure: "I just realized I'm competing with you. I don't want to do that. I really want to cooperate and see what we can do to solve this problem. Let me try again."

Saying words to that effect would be quite disarming to a spouse primed for further battle and would hopefully get the dialogue back to problem solving instead of war.

War in a marriage solves nothing. It only makes things worse. *No one* wins in a marriage war. If one seems to win, the other withdraws only for the purpose of figuring out how to punish the winner.

Never once have I said sincerely to Larry, "Thank you, my love, for pointing out my faults so completely. I appreciate, too, your guiding me as to what I should be thinking and doing. I shall try my hardest from now on to keep in mind how I might improve!"

Nor has he ever said it to me. What do we do instead? We dip into our bag of tricks of punishment techniques. These consist of manipulative behavior we've already found effective, like distancing, withdrawing, pouting, ignoring and other common behaviors.

One couple confessed to not having spoken to each other for six weeks! Finally, the husband held a sign around the corner of the kitchen that said, "Do you want to go to a movie?" The wife was ready to laugh and call a truce.

It's a great story, but it seems a lot of work to quit speaking for that long . . . indeed, for *any* length of time. The time spent in not speaking is an enormous drain on one's energy, not to mention the total lack of solution it affords.

So we might agree that we could use the time better in noncompetitive conversation that would be useful in at least three ways:

First, I get to express my feelings and not have to carry them around as heavy burdens for who knows how long.

Second, you know me better when you've gotten to hear what's on my mind. You have a constantly updated report on this spouse of yours. You know what I'm about, whether you like it or not.

Third, we now have an "agenda" on the table to attack together. We know where to focus some energy in order to make the problem disappear.

That all sounds so simple, and even as I write it I wonder why Larry and I aren't always able to operate that efficiently! Any two six-year-olds ought to be able to grasp these concepts and make them work, right? Wrong. I think I know why.

My self-esteem is not quite up to snuff, and neither is Larry's. Neither is anyone else's.

Of course, I don't know that for a fact. Perhaps there are a few blessed souls running around with near-perfect self-esteem, who are able to say to themselves, "Interesting that this person disapproves of me so strongly. I hope I can calmly help find the problem so that we might find a pleasant comradery together!"

Most of us go into code blue at the slightest negative comment and shift into irrational, wild-eyed, nonproductive behavior: tears, anger, whatever. We feel attacked and unworthwhile when someone registers any complaint that sounds as though we're to blame. Often our response has nothing to do with the facts, whether or not we *are* to blame. It has to do, instead, with our feelings as we hear the other person express something negative.

So many, many things go into any one remark a person might make. Let's pretend I wake up one morning feeling grumpy. I ate at bedtime, had a restless night, got awakened by a raucous bird outside my window at dawn, weighed three pounds more than I did yesterday, and thought again of the enormous ironing waiting for me after work. I shuffle out to the kitchen and, as I put my instant coffee into the microwave, I ask Larry, "You have a church meeting tonight?"

Now, granted, I've already established a reputation for resenting how many activities take up his evenings, but this morning I'm not looking for a fight. I only want to know his schedule.

He has awakened with a fierce backache from driving all day long, and a bank statement that wouldn't resolve with the checkbook late last night. He's looking for milk and finding only a tablespoon left in the milk carton. His favorite banana bread is all gone. He hears my question and with lightning speed interprets it as still another attack on his priorities.

"It's here on the calendar," he states a little more loudly than necessary considering we're standing only two feet apart. "It's been *on* the calendar for some four months. We meet *every* Tuesday night. This *is* Tuesday, right?"

"I know what night it is. I only thought that since you met last night maybe there wouldn't be a meeting tonight." My tone is hardly the sweet-voiced, tender-lover tone. And now I cast about for ammunition. "And you have a basketball game tomorrow night, right?"

"Right," he replies in ominous softness. "Is the banana bread all gone?"

"If it isn't there, it must be all gone," I say, implying that any ninny might figure that out.

In short, our morning is off to a rather dismal start. How can that be? We didn't want it to be this way. We're two pretty nice people who have high regard for one another, a lot of respect and caring, not to mention a 36-year relationship. Why are we trading arrows on this lovely morning?

Because of a lot of things. Because of poor sleep, too much work, headaches, backaches, no milk and no banana bread.

That, on top of my sensitivity to his moods and his to mine, gives us the makings of a nice little quarrel.

It doesn't mean we don't love each other. It means we're both experiencing some disappointments in living that are actually relatively unimportant. That's *all* it means. It has practically nothing to do with our marriage or with each other.

Those same feelings and thoughts, expressed between two people with high self-esteem, might stop at this point with a giggle. Both might look at the other, laugh, shake their heads and go about having a wonderful day.

But not so with people who aren't sure they're okay. We're so easily threatened by a perceived criticism that we lose perspective. I find myself wondering, "Does he prefer doing everything with other people? Doesn't he enjoy my company anymore? If I were different, somehow, maybe he'd want to spend more time with me. He knows me better than anyone else in the whole world, so if *he* sees me as faulty I must be. I should have bought milk. I should have made another banana bread. I should be better in bed. I spent too much time on the kids instead of on him." Behind my terse negative words lies a whole chicken house full of self-doubts and self-blames that, again, have very little to do with Larry or our marriage.

He is thinking, too. "Am *I* such a jerk? I try so hard to be a good husband. It's not like I chase women or drink or lie. But she's resentful of me and she used to love me so much. I've fallen short of her expectations. I can't seem to measure up anymore. I should have spent more on her birthday present, maybe. It's because I'm not good at fixing things. I should be better in bed. I wasn't involved enough with the kids. Damn! I just can't do it right."

I suspect we're like a lot of people . . . unsure of our own value and worth, and, therefore, much too quick to take almost any comment as a reminder of failure.

The crux of the problem, then, is self-doubt. That's what gets in the way of two reasonably intelligent adults being able to discuss and solve problems without pain. Ideally there should be no pain in problem solving. We have needs and wants. How can we help each other achieve them?

And, in fact, the process *is* simple in other relationships. When our friend Bill comes to work in the yard I can say, "Bill, these are my priorities: first trim the pyracantha, then the Texas ranger. The yucca has outgrown its pot; it needs to go in that barrel. Trim the ivy off the ground and rake up pine needles for as much time as you have left, okay?"

Bill might say, "The yucca won't do well in that barrel; it needs full sun."

"Oh. Okay, where shall we move the barrel?"

"How about here?"

"No, that's our route to the garbage cans. Maybe here?"

"That'll work."

"Great. Thanks."

Never once have Bill and I clashed or hurt each other emotionally. We're together for a common cause and we make decisions easily and efficiently. Work gets done, problems get solved. There are no hidden agendas.

Marriage is so loaded with hidden agendas, it's a wonder we survive it at all, let alone with any good grace.

We have so many fears and hurts left over from long ago, and they all live in our houses with us and our unsuspecting mates. We spouses often have no idea of the leftover garbage our wives and husbands are still dealing with.

A very common one is the issue of control.

One of my clients, Ian, is a dear, gentle man. He and Jill were treating themselves to some marriage counseling as their anniversary present, which I thought was a delightful idea for a gift. One issue we dealt with was Ian's anger at almost any request Jill made of him. What emerged was the resentment he still carried toward the control his late father had exercised over him. Dad had been a strong and dominant figure with little praise for Ian . . . mostly criticism. Ian never could measure up to Dad's expectations, and any work he did under Dad's orders was joyless and tense. He dreaded his father's demands and developed an anxiety about demands that carried over long after Dad was dead.

When Jill would ask Ian to do something, he inwardly cringed. No matter how nicely Jill phrased a request she saw Ian bristle and darken, and his mood become hostile. If he did the job, it was as tense and joyless as if he were minding his father some 40 years ago. He didn't understand it, and certainly Jill didn't. No wonder resentment cropped up between them, as any request she made started a cold war.

Ian was responding according to habit, and it was a habit of fear. Fear dictates a lot of negative behavior. So much so that at least one psychologist states that people feel basically only two feelings: love or fear. Gerald Jampolski, in his book *Love Is Letting Go Of Fear,*[1] believes that if we're not operating from love, we're operating from fear.

I recommended that book to Ian and Jill to help both

of them understand the old fears Ian was struggling with; being dominated and controlled, and feeling helpless and discouraged. Jill needed to see behind the anger and know its roots to deal with it effectively. Anger on her part only reinforced the fear in Ian, and the vicious circle was in motion. Gentleness and encouragement from her would eventually help him relax and learn there was nothing to be afraid of anymore. Previously her response to his anger was distancing herself; withdrawing and becoming preoccupied and chilly, which only served to remind him more of his disapproving father.

When we can understand each other's fears, it's a lot easier to take our mate's bad behavior as a symptom of their inadequacies rather than as an attack on us. Generally that's all it is.

Sometimes I think we're all like giant stuffed animals wearing ugly Halloween masks. Inside we're soft and cuddly, but we've acquired these masks in our childhood and we put them on to hide behind and/or scare "bad" people away. They're our defense, and sometimes we're afraid to take them off. Perhaps they serve us in the outside world; perhaps we might occasionally need them. But, really, I doubt that they serve us very well in *any* circumstance, and I know for sure they only hamper us in a marriage.

It's no fun for a teddy bear to cuddle up to another teddy bear who's wearing a monster mask.

What's the solution, then?

Turn the page.

1. Gerald Jampolsky, *Love is Letting Go of Fear,* New York, Bantam, 1979.

Chapter 7

Can We Talk?

Of all the possible solutions that will let two nice, soft teddy bears get rid of their monster masks and cuddle up to each other, there is only one that really works:

Communication.

To talk. To converse. To share feelings, fears, anxieties, hopes, dreams, memories and wishes. To express our wants.

Communication has two parts, though, and one of them often gets overlooked: listening. In some marriages one partner talks easily and unceasingly, but never stops to let the other person talk. One talks and the other listens, and that's almost as bad as nobody sharing.

Sometimes I suggest a kitchen timer for couples with this problem, and recommend that they use it for a while just to become aware of their patterns. One talks for five minutes, and when the timer dings, the other talks.

One wife complained that her husband talked too slowly, with such great long pauses between words that he said practically nothing before his five minutes were up. He joked about requiring the timing to be done like football or basketball, where the clock moves only when there is action going on. Talking for five minutes might take that man 15 minutes! He suggested taking seven minutes to her five, because it took him longer to think about what he wanted to say.

Anything can be accomplished when both people are looking to cooperate. *Nothing* can be accomplished when one or both are not cooperating.

What if you're a couple who already talks a lot, but still have long unresolved problems? You have to do what marriage counselors do: Find the short circuit in the connection.

When we seem unable to arrive at new workable solutions, we need to see clearly what approaches we've tried so we can shift gears and try a different approach. Most of us tend to find a favorite tactic and stick with it come hell or high water. (Never mind that it hasn't helped yet; it *should* work!)

"I've told him and told him to pick up his dirty laundry, but do you think he ever does it on his own? No! I have to keep telling him!"

That kind of technique is more common than you would believe. We tell and tell, remind a thousand times, and tell some more, all the while complaining that we shouldn't have to remind.

We *don't* have to remind. Of course we can continue that process for the rest of our married lives if it suits us. But we need to be forewarned that the bad behavior will continue just as long. No one is going to change his or her behavior just because someone says to change it.

So what happens if a wife decides not to keep on with the first option of reminding her husband to pick up his clothes?

Option Number Two could be deciding that it isn't worth the hassle. She'll just pick up the dirty laundry herself and save her breath. But she'll probably be mad as a hornet and punish him in some other way.

Option Number Three might be an honest explanation of how his habit makes her feel, and a request for help in solving it. "Sweetie, when you leave your dirty laundry on the floor I feel really annoyed (or miffed, exasperated, disappointed, resentful, angry or whatever fits best) because I don't want to pick it up, nor do I want to keep reminding you. When can we talk about this issue?"

That's one of my favorite tried-and-true formulas for opening discussions that need to be had. "When you . . . I feel . . . because . . . ." It's not guaranteed to be effective, and I can't promise that the other party won't get angry, but it's the most respectful confrontation I know of, and you must start somewhere. Here are some examples:

"When you get upset at my every request I feel very sorry for myself because it gets in the way of finding solutions or compromises."

"When you scold the kids at the dinner table I feel sorry for them and mad at you because dinner should be a pleasant time for us."

"When you forget my birthday I'm devastated because it's the one day of the year I want to be treated very specially."

"When you make jokes about my weight in front of guests I get furious because it's cruel to embarrass someone."

Wouldn't it be grand if simply uttering those words would insure that your spouse would never again stoop to such dastardly deeds? No such luck—it's just the beginning. But every solution needs a beginning in order to proceed to a finish.

That statement "When you . . . I feel . . . because . . . ." is my favorite beginning. It doesn't even have to proceed to the next step. Using that statement is like dipping your toe into the pool to test the water. You can test to see if your partner is receptive to some respectful, honest communication.

Just because one person is ready to talk doesn't necessarily mean the other is. And if the temperature isn't right, good sense tells us to back off—but only temporarily. Too often we back off altogether and never resume the conversation that really needs to be had.

For example, someone might say, "Hey, I *told* her I don't like the way she corrects me when I'm telling something to our friends, but she got mad right away and that was the end of that."

We tend to let things "end" prematurely when they're not really ended. We're still carrying around unresolved anger and hostility.

We positively must communicate as long as it takes to reach some resolution, but it doesn't have to be all at once! There is no time limit. We can solve a difference of opinion in one minute or one month or 20 years, but the important thing is to continue working on it. We get defeated too easily. Persistence is essential, but so is consideration for the other's feelings—honesty with kindness.

If the man is in bed with the flu and a raging fever, that's not a good time for the woman to say, "When you interrupt me I feel annoyed because you seem to think what I'm saying is not important."

She's a hundred percent right in making that statement, but it can't get far in the face of the flu. Hopefully she'll broach it when he's feeling better.

Even then, we can be pretty sure he won't say, "Why, darling girl, thanks for telling me. I was a beast to do that. It'll never happen again." Life just is not that easy! He might, however, be receptive to communicating and say,

"I didn't know I ever interrupted you. When did I do that?"

The temptation might be for her to answer, "You *always* do that," because she may have been keenly aware of it many times. But few things happen "always," and exaggerating won't help solve the problem.

A specific incident would help. "Last night when your sister was here and I was telling her how I make raspberry vinaigrette, you just started showing her that new book you bought."

He might apologize, which would be lovely, and the whole issue can be dropped. But let's say he doesn't. He might excuse his behavior with, "I thought you were through."

"I wasn't."

Now is a good time for her to "ask for the sale." To define what she wants from him. "At any rate, could we agree that neither of us will interrupt the other one?"

"Sure."

"Great. Thanks."

That's how communication *could* happen. Wouldn't it be grand to get things taken care of so quickly? But you and I both know that too often things don't go that smoothly.

What if he had bristled and attacked with, "I suppose you think you never interrupt me?" or "Well, maybe if you wouldn't talk nonstop all the time I wouldn't have to interrupt," or "Nobody cares about your vinegar anyway," or "Oh, boy, here we go again. I never do anything right, do I?" or "What is this, lecture number 94?" or something like that. There are millions of snappy retorts along those lines, and we've all heard them many times.

That retort is a cue that the pool water is not the right temperature. He is not going to be a cooperative communicator, or so it appears. She might try again.

"Look, I'm trying to be respectful and tell you my feelings about something that's important to me. Would you be respectful, too, and not get sarcastic?"

If that's said in a quietly calm voice there is a chance he'll back off and be more open to cooperation. If so, great—go ahead. If not, define feelings again.

"When you refuse to discuss problems I feel really discouraged because we'll never get our differences settled unless we talk about them. But I'm certainly willing to wait until later to talk about it. When *can* we talk about it?"

"Why do we have to talk about problems all the time? You make life so unpleasant."

"I just want to settle this one problem if we can. How about after dinner? Tonight? Tomorrow? You decide."

That's a respectful way to approach a person who wants to avoid discussing unpleasant subjects (which includes a large part of the population, by the way). Sometimes it elicits an, "Oh, well, let's talk about it now." But sometimes not. The point is, we have to be persistent if we're dealing with someone who prefers to avoid uncomfortable issues.

It's doing no favor to anyone to sigh, martyr-like, and say with resignation, "Oh, never mind. It wouldn't do any good anyway." We can't let ourselves have the luxury of "letting it go" and feeling superior. That just enables us to chalk up another unresolved hurt and heap another coal on the fire of resentment. We *have* to keep trying if we're to have any hope of improving our relationship.

By the time people are old enough to marry they've established patterns that are so deeply imbedded it can be awfully hard to change them. Indeed they can *seem* impossible to change. We need to keep reminding ourselves that it is truly impossible for us to change our mates . . . we can change only ourselves. But they certainly have the capacity to change themselves, if they choose to.

If they choose to. That's a biggie.

If my behavior is working for me, getting all my needs met and/or avoiding unpleasant issues, then I'm probably not going to want to change. Change comes only when my discomfort is sufficient to warrant it.

That's why the wife who complains, "I've told him and told him and told him to pick up his dirty laundry," is still having to pick it up herself. Her husband, that smart man, discovered long ago that he can survive the barrage of reminders very well. And, it's a small price to pay for getting out of picking up his dirty clothes. Why should he change? To him the end result would be negative, not positive. He likes it better this way.

For him to even *want* to change, there would have to be a good reason. How can his wife find a reason?

Honesty, communication and persistence. Being perfectly honest and nonmanipulative, she would express her feelings. "Honey, I'm tired of being a nag. I am quitting as of this minute telling you to pick up your dirty laundry. That has to be your decision. In fact, I apologize for nagging you about it all these months (or years). But I won't pick it up, either, because if I did I'd get resentful and punish you in some other way. I'll wash anything that's in the hamper. So, if your clothes aren't there they'll just stay dirty, okay?"

My guess is the husband would be so delighted to hear this he'd grin broadly and say, "Great, doll!" and maybe even give her a smooch.

She could feel a marvelous sense of freedom from this annoying nuisance to which she'd chained herself all that time. She returns his affection with enthusiasm, knowing she's no longer responsible for his laundry.

Let's imagine the scenario. As the days go by their bedroom becomes strewn with dirty shirts, pants, socks, underwear, running shorts, swimming trunks and sweaty headbands.

She's keenly aware of the rising heaps of mounting laundry, but she's unaffected. She just watches the process occur.

One or two hitches might happen, like when he says, "Babe, I need a white shirt for the banquet tonight, and they're all dirty. Can you wash one for me?"

Her immediate response might be, "No white shirts? Whose fault is that? You'd have white shirts if you'd just dropped them in the hamper. But no, you can't be bothered with details like that. See what happens when I turn over some responsibility to you? Ha! Now you know why I told you and told you to pick up your laundry. You are so helpless! I can't believe you've let all these clothes pile up. What a slob."

But if she indulges in that tirade, it means she hasn't changed herself. She's just put her feelings on temporary hold. If she *has* changed, she would see it very differently. She is no longer responsible. It's his problem. He's quite able to figure out for himself a few options that will get him through, but that's his job, not hers.

If I were she I'd say something like, "Oh, that's too bad they're all dirty. No, I'm not washing clothes today; I have a lot of other things to do." And I'd leave the room. No need standing there to hash it all over. No need to make suggestions, like "Maybe you could buy a new white shirt today." He can think of that all by himself. Or he can dig through the pile and pull out a dirty white shirt to wear to the banquet. That's his right.

If she thinks, "I can't stand being with him at the banquet if he's wearing a dirty shirt," she has the right to stay home. However, chances are she could stand it very well.

He might get angry with her for not having the shirt clean, but he has full rights to any feelings he chooses to indulge in, and she can stand that, too.

Now, the process of change has just begun, and there are still a myriad of details to work out. I know wives reading this are thinking, "Yeah, my husband would stack up dirty clothes until he ran out of things to wear, then dump them all in the wash at once. It would take me two solid days of doing laundry to catch up. No thanks!"

One of the options there is this: "Love, I need to tell you my feelings about your dirty clothes. I'm not willing to have a giant stack of them dumped in the hamper all at once for me to spend two days working on. I know you don't like picking them up as you go along, and I don't like being responsible for them. We need to find other ways to handle this. Do you have any suggestions?"

Asking our mates for their input is often amazingly effective. When we're part of the solution, we're way more willing to cooperate than when someone makes decisions for us.

Another option is this: "I don't want to wash more than two loads a week (or whatever is appropriate). How about doing your own laundry? Then you can let it pile up as long as you want."

That means letting him handle it *any* way he wants. One wife reported that her husband opted to take it all to a laundry once a month and the bill was enormous. We have to be willing to let that happen. We can't have control of our spouse's behavior. There will always be things we disapprove of, and money spent is a big issue. But still there has been a change in behavior, which is what we're looking for.

This is not manipulation because it's up-front and honest.

It's not game playing. It's simply defining what I will and will not do.

There are many other variations on this course of action, and you might want to talk about them together. It's not a technique that's meant to cause more resentment. Conversing about it is permissible and even advisable, so long as it's not the old routine of "telling him and telling him."

It might include: "Sweetie, this bedroom is getting a dreadful stench about it from your sweaty laundry. I'm having trouble sleeping in here. Maybe you could move your stuff out to the back porch or garage or basement, or I could sleep in the guest room . . . you decide."

I love the phrase "you decide." It gives a lot of freedom to the other person, and it's very respectful. I can tell you my decisions in the matter and you can decide what you prefer.

One very big caution, however, is letting this method become a power struggle. Marriages can end over both parties becoming so determined to win that solution-finding takes a back seat to battle strategies.

Remember: *Nobody wins in a power struggle.* The focus should be strictly on finding an acceptable resolution, not on punishing the guilty party.

Getting into a power struggle is just one way of short-circuiting the communication process. We need to keep an eye out for any short circuit that prevents resolution. The most frequent offenders are these:

1. Judging the other person as "bad" and/or "wrong," and therefore deserving of punishment.

Instead, take the approach that we have a common problem or difference between us that needs to be solved.

2. Going for a victory, being determined to "win."

Instead we need to focus on cooperating, not competing. We stand a much better chance of working through every difficulty when we work together. Power struggles only serve to divide us further.

3. Manipulating, trying to change the other's attitudes and/or behavior by using our emotions to affect their feelings.

Instead we need to talk *and* listen, for as long as it takes (though it doesn't have to be nonstop) with honest disclosures of feelings and hopes, defining what we'd like.

4. Withdrawing, distancing, refusing to get involved at all. This may be the most powerful position of all. It's impossible for the spouse of a close-mouthed, totally noncommunicative person to achieve any kind of resolution. Although we may judge the silent person as "weak," we must recognize the relentless strength demonstrated by refusing to talk, which leaves the other partner nearly helpless.

Instead we need to be willing to communicate respectfully, in order to maintain *any* relationship!

There are, no doubt, many variations on all those faulty circuits, and probably many other flaws I haven't defined. But these are the ones I come across most often in my practice.

Fighting is one of the biggest wastes of time and energy. When there is fighting, there is a power struggle. And nobody wins in a power struggle.

I know there are a lot of people who will disagree with me that fighting is wasteful. They usually protest, "But it's unhealthy to keep anger inside. When you're upset you have to let it all out." Sometimes they even add, "Otherwise you might get cancer."

I agree that bottling up anger is unhealthy. So how do we release anger without fighting? It can be done very effectively, and it doesn't need an audience. In fact, you can yell and scream and holler all alone and enjoy feeling free and uninhibited by spectators.

There are many things we do best when we're alone; going to the bathroom, for one thing. It's important for good health, but it's accomplished best without observers.

Releasing anger falls in the same category. If you think it's good for you, by all means, enjoy the process. But don't expect anyone to stay in the room with you.

I maintain that nothing can be settled or resolved in the heat of emotion. There are two different areas of need (and I use the word "need" loosely) that we often mistakenly pursue at the same time; the need to express emotion and the need to solve a problem.

It may sound like an efficient use of time to work on both needs concurrently, but it just isn't effective. The problem-solving gets shoved aside in the face of the emotion-releasing.

I tell my clients this: As soon as one of you raises your voice in anger or starts to cry, then shelve the issue you're working on. Leave the room and allow your feelings to surface. Cry as long and hard as you feel like crying. Or, kick the tree, run furiously around the block six times, beat on a mattress or shout cuss words in your basement; but give in thoroughly to venting emotion until you're spent.

Then. Blow your nose, bandage your foot (where you kicked the tree), have a nice drink of water and come back to the conversation. With clear minds and healthy bodies you can again look for solutions. But the minute either person feels tears or anger welling up, repeat the process.

"You have to be kidding," clients say. "That would take forever."

So? There is no rush. Trying to find understanding or compassion or answers would take forever, too, in the face of anger or tears—and any solutions you *did* find would probably be less than satisfactory.

You wouldn't try to wash your car and make an omelet at the same time. Both are worthy activities, but they can't be done simultaneously. Once we recognize that it's logical to separate anger-releasing from problem-solving, we can incorporate that same thinking in our communication.

It might be difficult at first, but that's okay. There is no rush. When either of you can remember to try the new process, you'll gradually find it gets easier.

The danger, now, is that the one who remembers you can't do both things at once might want to lord it over the other one. "Nyaa, nyaa, nyaa, Lee Schnebly says we can't talk if one person is crying or shouting, so I'm going to the movies, nyaa, nyaa." It could become just one more form of manipulation or power or withdrawal. Isn't it amazing how many ways we can find to mess up a relationship?

I know my beliefs will be vehemently rejected by many people who believe down to their toes that fighting is good. They feel cleansed by a good heated exchange, and it has, in fact, enhanced their marriages. I never argue with success. If you're one of those people who enjoys a good scrap and you're married to another, you have my sincere blessings and admiration for taking a behavior that could be destructive and making it a positive force in your lives. Don't even *consider* changing if you're both enjoying your relationship the way it is.

The suggestions I make are for people whose lives together aren't working the way they want them to. My views on fighting are based on the feelings I have when someone verbally attacks me and anger surges up as a result. In that state I've never felt a desire to cooperate and lovingly search for compromise and understanding. I doubt that many people feel much differently. Anger begets anger.

But that's not to say that I believe in being a wimp and pussyfooting around an uncomfortable situation. Acting like everything is fine when you're a churning mass of hurt or anger inside would be even more damaging than a temper tantrum.

I guess the element I think of as being most important is *respect*. I want to tell you what's wrong in my life. I want you to know what you did that disappointed me. You deserve to hear what I would like in place of that behavior. You need to know what makes me sad, mad, glad or scared if we're to have a good working relationship. But I want to tell you all those things in a respectful way, not an attacking way. Attacks hurt, and I don't want to hurt anyone—especially the people I live with.

It's perfectly appropriate to say, "I am so angry right now that I don't want to try to talk about it. I'd say hurtful things. Let me cool down a while, then I'll be able to talk rationally."

The same is true if I'm crying. It's fine to say, "Boo hoo, sob sob . . . Let me cry for a while and *then* we can talk, sniff sniff."

A marvelous way of discovering what causes the short circuits in your own patterns of communication is to tape-record your conversations. Larry and I tried that once, and it got so funny we finally laughed and stopped the recorder. Both of us were being so careful to talk "right" that we weren't being ourselves at all. We were caught up in jargon like, "Do I hear you saying that . . ." and "I can't argue with your feelings, but my belief is . . . ."

Playing it back, we roared at the phoniness of the dialogue, but we certainly had been in good control of ourselves.

You probably don't need a tape recorder. You already know who gets mad and yells, who cries, who withdraws, who uses sarcasm, etc. All you need to do now is decide to switch that behavior for a new kind.

Sometimes it's fun to switch roles. You both do what the other one normally does. The crier now yells and screams. The yeller cries or doesn't respond . . . all in the name of scientific experimentation. Of course nothing gets straightened out that way, but it does shed light on the other person's feelings. That's worth something.

We need to keep in mind, however, that getting our needs met is a lifelong process. Few of us ever get to say, "There now. My needs in this relationship are all met, and there they'll stay."

It would be easier if we didn't change so much, but we do. What I wanted in a mate at 20 is a far cry from what I want now. And I suspect my ideals will continue changing to my grave.

The positive thought, though, is that the skills we develop in *getting* our needs met will be useful every day. Like riding a bike, we'll never forget how. Unlike riding a bike, we're called upon to use these skills constantly, so they should keep sharpening themselves. I haven't been on a bike in some 15 years, but I converse daily.

Sometimes people ask Larry, "Doesn't it drive you crazy to be married to a counselor? She must know all the tricks."

Sometimes Larry has agreed with fervent desperation. Many times both of us have wondered if our marriage was the right one. Would life have been easier if we'd married someone else?

Both of us (fortunately) agree that it probably wouldn't have. We'd have different spouses with different problems to deal with, but we'd still have problems. Marriage is just hard, that's all. But not impossibly hard. Maybe we should be glad it's so challenging, because it demands that we keep growing.

Sometimes I compare it to two rough stones put into a rock polisher. The very abrasiveness of the process makes the rocks smooth and shiny, and much more beautiful than they were before.

There are no "tricks" to a happy marriage, but there are some skills that can help make the process much less frustrating and more productive. All of them have the same base:

Being willing to communicate with honesty and respect. That's it in a nutshell.

Chapter 8

Sex
in Marriage

Cinderella never had sex. She got all dressed up, went to the ball and charmed the socks off the handsome prince, who whisked her off to the castle. Then for the rest of their lives, he worshipped her, agreed with her, hugged her often, kissed her tenderly, held her close as they talked hour after hour, chuckled warmly at her cute ways and made her happy. She was the princess. He was the prince put into this world to make her happy ever after!

Though that concept may be a bit ridiculous, many women unconsciously expect marriage to be that way. Most of us were totally unaware of the expectations our husbands had been entertaining. While we were fantasizing about being Cinderella in the castle, the boys were busy with their own fantasies. In theirs, Cinderella was a real sexpot. She couldn't wait to hop off the horse, race the prince to the castle garret and begin an outrageous strip-tease to the tune of Harlem Nocturne. That was only the beginning of the passionate sex life they would enjoy forevermore, in which she couldn't keep her hands off his body. She would be his own Playboy bunny—aggressive, seductive and sultry. She would combine these traits with others that would be helpful to his career. She would also be a gourmet cook, a kind of combination Farrah Fawcett and Julia Child.

Because today's young wives see love, sex and marriage far differently from the way their mothers viewed them, we might think young women sail into marriage with nary a misconception. But alas, it doesn't work that way. Cinderella and the prince live on in a never-ending clash of "shoulds" that both partners still bring to the wedding.

Our expectations are part of the problem. One is the old appeal of forbidden fruit. All of us want what we can't have. Conversely we often *don't* want what we *should* have. Recently, a bride of less than a year poured out her hurt and confusion in my office. "Tom and I couldn't get enough sex before we were married. We slept together the first night we met and several times a day after that. We lived in his apartment for four months before the wedding. Our sex life was unbelievable. But right after we got married, he cooled almost immediately. Now he hardly touches me!"

Tom said, "If Margie would just quit hounding me for sex, I probably would want her again. But by now it's such a big 'should' that it's no fun. The more she nags me, the more I turn off."

Tom and Margie came from religious homes. Both felt guilty, even while their enjoyed their fantastic premarital sex. Once it was approved, it lost much of its appeal for Tom. Some people love a challenge. When the challenge goes, so does the lust. Furthermore, it became a power struggle to each of them. Each tried to make the other behave in the way they "should."

Couples who remain virgins until the marriage bed sometimes feel disappointed after "saving" themselves all that time while they read about the fireworks that awaited them. Sometimes the actual experience doesn't measure up to the almost-unbearable ecstasy they imagined. They feel cheated, discouraged and angry with each other.

"It just isn't as exciting as I thought it would be," they say.

The very intimacy of marriage can also detract from sexual desire. The dashing young man who visits Pam in her singles apartment is pure excitement with his flowers, gifts and bottles of good wine. The scent of his shave lotion thrills her, as does his sparkling conversation and even the tone of his voice. His touch is magic and his gaze electric. Simply being in his presence is an automatic turn-on. The thrill of his kisses makes him totally irresistible. The physical attraction is constant and insatiable.

Then comes the wedding and the total togetherness and the beginning of disillusionment. Pam begins to resent little habits she wasn't aware of before. She misses the flowers, gifts and bottles of wine. There are few surprises anymore. There's criticism, arguing and disapproval. His touch is no longer an automatic turn-on, but a demand. She bristles at it sometimes.

Though the pilot light is not necessarily out, it is definitely flickering.

Our grandmothers used to say, "Familiarity breeds contempt." Only determined couples can keep sex fun and exciting in spite of constant familiarity. Most of us thought it would be fun and exciting forever, or we wouldn't have agreed to marry in the first place. Is there a solution? I don't think so.

Maybe disillusionment is part of a giant Master Plan to

keep civilization going. Maybe we need our naive attitude of hope and expectation or no one would ever marry. But whether or not we need it, I'm convinced we'll always have it. Hope springs eternal.

Our expectations cause us some disappointment. So what? Sex is no different from anything else. As we live and grow, we discover many expectations can cause us disappointment. It's one of those lessons we learn only by experiencing it frequently enough.

Another problem in sexuality is the variety of different needs we have. So many disenchanted young wives tell me, "All he thinks of is sex! I want to be held and kissed and hugged. But for him, it always leads to the bedroom. I want *love,* but he just wants *sex."*

The husbands look confused and say, "Isn't that what marriage is for? Of course I want sex. Adults who love each other should want sex. I love my wife. I just can't understand her not wanting sex as much as I do."

I think they're both right. There's a lot of truth to the statement, "Men use love to get sex and women use sex to get love." Of course women enjoy good sex and men genuinely love their wives. But I think the thrust of their focus is biologically different.

Often a wife will express a wish to be simply held, "with no strings attached." She doesn't want sex—only a gentle tenderness that will make her feel close and loved. And the husband will shrug and say, "Well, sure, if that's all she wants, I can do that. I'll be glad just to hold her with no strings attached." And he means it sincerely. He loves his wife, and if it will make her happy he's glad to oblige.

Later that evening he joins her on the sofa just to hold her. She's delighted! She snuggles warmly and thinks, "This is what life is all about. Oh, this is lovely! I feel so warm, secure, content and loved!" And just about then she feels his hand on her breast, hears his breathing get heavy and sees hunger in his eyes. A stab of resentment goes through her. He promised! He said no strings attached, and now he wants to go to bed. No fair! She pulls away in disappointment, sees the rejection and hurt in his face, and she feels guilty.

Sometimes she goes ahead with it and they have sex. But she feels cheated of the pure, undemanding tenderness she had expected him to provide. Or, she may refuse sex and he feels rejected, unloved, hurt and angry. Either or both end up unhappy.

What happens? They may begin to avoid these situations to avoid the potential hurt. The wife may find any number of chores to do in the evening so she won't appear idle and inviting. The husband may hesitate to make any overtures at all rather than risk rejection. Both feel like failures. They're just two normal people with feelings like everyone else. The problem is that one has a quicker turn-on point than the other.

It can work both ways. I've encountered more women who complain of overly ardent husbands. But many women complain their husbands won't turn on no matter how flimsy their nightgowns or how many hints they toss out.

I'm convinced one partner or the other always has a higher sex drive. So what's the big deal? Why is it any worse if one has a bigger appetite than the other?

It's all right for a couple to go to dinner and order what they want. For him, a giant slab of prime rib complete with baked potato, sour cream, fried zucchini, salad with roquefort dressing, garlic bread and apple pie with ice cream. For her, a chef's salad. We never question the difference in food appetites, but somehow we feel there's something wrong if our sexual appetites differ.

We believe if we really love each other, we should both want to make love at the same instant, with the same regularity. And if we don't, we feel angry, guilty, hurt—or all three.

It seems to me the obvious solution is to think of sex the way we think of food. If Larry loves rice pudding every night and I don't, nothing prevents me from fixing it for him. I'll be glad to give him rice pudding frequently, if he wants it, as long as he doesn't insist I have some, too. From time to time I might decide rice pudding looks pretty good and I'll have a dish myself. But you can be sure if he *demands* rice pudding or lays a guilt trip on me because I don't want any, I may starve to death before I'll eat any. I may even stop providing it for him.

Some good friends of ours have been married for 35 years. They handle the "problem" of differing sexual appetites so well it never became a problem at all. They simply agreed years ago their only obligation to each other was to "be there." Frequently, when one's desire is greater than the other's, both end up equally excited by just being there. If they don't, that's fine. One can be actively thrilled, and the other simply pleased at cooperating. Feelings don't get hurt and egos don't get shattered because neither has any expectations or "shoulds."

Not infrequently my clients, almost always the women, complain they feel "used." Trudy said, "I stay home with the kids all day, and my only contact with the outside world might be other women at a plastic-ware party or a neighbor's coffee. Mike is at a huge office full of people all day long. Some of the women he talks to are gorgeous. I know he likes them. I feel like he gets turned on by them all day long, then comes home and expects me to satisfy all that desire. It's not love for me he's feeling, just pure physical lust for something feminine. I'm supposed to be available. Not only available, but willing and eager. Well, I'm sorry, but I'm not."

Mike denies the accusation, but his reassurances fall on deaf ears. It's possible Trudy is at least partly right because sometimes we do get excited by people other than our mates. We automatically turn to our mates without even questioning where the desire came from in the first place.

This won't be a problem if other things are going well. If there's an atmosphere of love, respect and cooperation to begin with, the lovemaking feels natural and good to both parties. But if the communication and warmth are lacking, sex becomes questionable.

Actually, sex is communication. When the communication is bad, sex is bad. When we improve our communication, we improve our sex lives.

Another fly in the ointment of sexuality is unexpressed resentment. I know from experience if I get angry with Larry and try to ignore it, pretend it isn't there and refuse to deal with it, I store up resentment until wild horses couldn't drag me to his arms. Until the issue is resolved, I will be a very reluctant bed partner, if at all. I'd be like my friend Betty who, when her husband makes unwelcome overtures, says, "Oh, you wanta play rent-a-corpse tonight?" Making love with a cold, grim wife is hardly rewarding, although lots of men prefer it to the alternative of no sex at all.

Another problem about unexpressed resentment is it increases the chance of an affair. The longer I withhold my feelings from Larry, the more appealing it becomes to share those feelings with someone else. I become vulnerable and so does he. A kind, sensitive ear from someone else is often an irresistible invitation to something more. Actually, I use the word "irresistible" very loosely because

I believe we *can* resist anything we want to resist. If we really want it, we like to convince ourselves we "just couldn't help it!"

Some people deliberately seek affairs to get even with their mates, as Marsha did. "I resented him so long and so hard I had an affair just to show him I wasn't going to put up with his lack of attention. I wanted to hurt him badly. I knew it would hurt him more than anything else."

She was right. It did. The relationship was irreparably damaged, which was more than Marsha had intended.

Unresolved resentment takes its toll in a lot of other unsavory ways, including lack of desire; even impotence. When I work with an impotent husband, I almost always find some hostility toward his wife that needs to be resolved before the physical problem can be solved.

One husband maintained he couldn't have an erection with his wife, but he often awoke with one. Being able to have an erection at *any* time means impotence is not a physical impairment. We had to look at his relationship with his wife. Once we improved their communication and the quality of time they spent together, his impotence disappeared.

Unresolved resentment almost always interferes with good sex. People who are "pleasers" need everyone's approval so much they don't express their irritations. They don't get angry. They get even. What better way to punish the offending spouse than by disinterest in sex?

The best solution to unresolved resentment is letting our feelings out. I *have* to tell Larry when I'm annoyed, disappointed or furious with him, even though I risk an argument, withdrawal or whatever made me reluctant to rock the boat in the first place. If I remind myself I can stand his disapproval, our relationship will benefit from my honest complaints. I find it helps me to talk things out and get it over with. The longer I put off talking to him honestly, the longer I have no desire for closeness, warmth or sex.

Although sex is one of the last things that should ever become a power arena, it frequently does. Carol complains, "Sex seems like a victory to him. It's like he's *won,* and I've lost. Even when he does nice things, I can see he's really just trying a gimmick so I'll give in. And when I do give in, I feel horrible afterward. I lie there and cry. I wonder why it isn't beautiful and rewarding anymore. Instead I'm just a challenge to his manhood. He proves he's macho by making love to me."

Though Carol could be misinterpreting her husband's intentions, chances are she's partially correct. We feel other people's attempts at power, although sometimes we don't recognize it as such. We just know it makes us mad.

"Oughta wantas" are big in the sexual battleground. "You oughta wanta make love. Wives oughta wanta have sex," he says. She counters with, "You oughta wanta talk to me. You oughta wanta be close to me."

When each tries to control the other, nobody wins. Everyone loses in a power struggle. If you "win," it's only a temporary victory until the other party bests you. Yet, tonight in millions of bedrooms around the world, people will compete, try to control one another and try to be more powerful by demanding or refusing sex.

The solution is to ask yourself if you're involved with that game. Sex and power can't survive simultaneously. Even in harmless games, like Monopoly or Scrabble, players often are sore losers. If you shoot for power in the bedroom, you automatically lose before you start.

How do you end the power struggle? One partner must be willing to withdraw from it. Share this insight with your partner, opening the subject for discussion. If that's too threatening, try changing your attitude, motivation and behavior.

Competition and cooperation cannot coexist at the same time. A rich sexual relationship demands cooperation. If you tend to be a competitive person, you may be competing in your marriage or love relationship. If you are, your sex life is probably disconcerting. Make the decision to start cooperating instead. Treat your partner with respect, improve your communication and get out of the one-upmanship game.

Sue and Andy came for counseling because their sex life was not what they wanted. "Sue seems to have a plastic shield around her," Andy complained. "She's fine when we're out for the evening with other people. She seems warm and happy. She even has a good time with me . . . until we reach our bedroom. Then she gets quiet, seems preoccupied and withdraws from me completely. She builds this wall around herself."

Sue nodded in agreement, with a very sad expression. She seemed to be taking the blame, but couldn't help what she was doing and felt bad about it.

We talked at length about feelings and attitudes. She told of her biggest fear. "I'm scared to death of being abandoned or rejected. I'll never forget the day my father walked out on my mother and how we all cried. Mother never got over it because she and my father had always been close. It came like a bolt from the blue. We had all trusted my father and we shouldn't have. He left us."

Sue's childhood decision was never to get into that bind herself. She avoided the risk by never getting too close to anyone.

But for sex to be good, there has to be trust. True, we're vulnerable when we trust. And some people prefer not to take that risk.

In Sue's case we had to do some counseling before she became willing to take the risk. Once the decision was reached, she was able to let down her defenses and open up to Andy for the first time since they'd married.

Sometimes the reason for distrust is more recent and very clear. "I was married before, and my first husband wasn't trustworthy. He was fooling around with other women right from the start. Our marriage was just a handy place to come between affairs."

It's a fact: There are no guarantees in this world. We're always vulnerable to deceit or a change of heart that could lead to rejection. If that happens, we can stand it. Yet a lot of people are reluctant to believe in anything that chancy. Ages ago someone said, "It's better to have loved and lost than never to have loved at *all*." But tell that to a recent divorcee and watch her expression of disdain.

It boils down to an individual decision, one we must all make for ourselves. Without a willingness to risk, to open up and be vulnerable, you'll never allow yourself to feel close to someone. Your sex life will be mediocre at best.

Personally, I highly recommend the risk. When you love someone, you are vulnerable. You'll be hurt from time to time, but it's worth it when you're able to enjoy a really intimate relationship.

Probably the all-time king-size problem in the sexual arena is performance. We worry about how our partner is going to evaluate us and whether or not we'll measure up to his or her expectations. What a shame anything so basic as sex has taken on so many fears of inadequacy. But it has. We experience fear of performance more than any other area of sexual dysfunction.

Debbie says plaintively, "The more educated we become, the more performance is demanded of us! It used to be that men were happy if their wives would 'just submit.' No more! Now they get upset and uptight if we don't have orgasms every time. Multiple orgasms, yet!

"They analyze our orgasms. My husband keeps asking, 'Did you have a vaginal orgasm or just a clitoral orgasm?' I'm sick of having my lovemaking analyzed all the time. I wish I could get away with 'just submitting' like my mother did!"

She has a realistic complaint. A husband may feel threatened if he can't send his wife into "webs of ecstasy," as a gothic novel might say. He is so concerned with perfection in lovemaking he may put pressure on his wife. This needlessly complicates the whole matter.

On a recent popular talk show, guests explained their research indicating women might be able to ejaculate during intercourse. While the largely feminine audience was interested in the presentation, one well-received comment was that now men will have yet another goal to pursue—finding the "magic button" to push so women could ejaculate.

"They've taken the magic out of romantic love," sighed one lady. "It's become a scientific skill." Someone else suggested what we need is more candlelight and wine, and fewer charts to follow. There was a feeling men and women already have far too many "shoulds" around intercourse.

Perhaps the biggest culprit behind our performance fears is the monster of perfectionism. "If I can't do something perfectly, I'm not going to try it at all." That attitude is crippling enough in other areas to cheat us out of a lot of pleasure, from reluctance to try new sports or new skills like guitar playing to sex. But sex never has to be perfect to be enjoyable.

I love my friend George's statement, "When sex is

good, it's just great. When sex is bad, it's still great!" George's wife is a lucky lady, with no pressures of performance and no expectations of perfection from her husband. George himself is equally lucky, with the freedom simply to enjoy and cooperate without measuring.

Once we start to measure the quality of our performance, we lose much of the pure pleasure we could be relishing. When we spend so much mental energy evaluating, we forfeit spontaneity.

But the worst penalty of perfectionistic evaluation is the fact we can *never* measure up! True perfection is impossible. We're doomed to a life of disappointment.

We need to lower our standards and apply the adage, "Have the courage to be imperfect." Quit worrying about performance. If you have to ask "How was it?" you're missing the whole point. As George says, "The worst sex I ever had was terrific!"

I'm not opposed to education, but I do think we might be taking sex education for adults a bit too seriously. There are thousands of cookbooks packed with jillions of mouth-watering recipes, but no husband ever expected us to try them all. In fact, most are content with a basic pot roast, potatoes, vegetable, bread and dessert. They rarely ask, "Aren't you willing to try the Pork-and-Apple Oriental on page 68 of that new cookbook you got for your birthday?" And if any husband did ask, the answer would likely be a resounding "No!" which would end the discussion then and there.

Not so with sex. "Dan says he and his wife read *The Delights of Sex* at bedtime and try a different page every night. Shall we do that?" Or "Honey, you're so conservative. There are hundreds of different positions. Why do you always want the same one or two or three?"

A wife might say, "My friend Julie can't wait 'til bedtime

because Steve is so creative in his lovemaking. He thinks of such exciting erotic things to do she just can't get enough!" Or, "I love reading those romantic novels because the sex scenes sound really fantastic. Why don't we make love that way?"

The resulting feelings are the same for both sexes—threat and inadequacy. "I must be a lousy lover. I'm dull, uncreative, stodgy. I'm a miserable failure and will avoid the whole thing." Another way of responding might be, "Damn it, if I'm not a good enough lover at home, I'll have an affair and prove I'm terrific." Regardless of which gender is complaining, the reaction is the same. "Maybe I can't measure up." So in self-defense, we attack each other.

"You know what you are? Frigid!"

"If you were a decent lover I'd be fine!" Then both partners feel threatened by their "poor performance," which in reality might be perfectly good.

We're the best-educated generation there ever was. A price we pay for it is the awareness anything can be improved. So we begin to feel inadequate. But education isn't the only cause. Plain old inferiority can also cause feelings of inadequacy.

"I have such small breasts. I'm ashamed to have my lover see them."

"I haven't had the experience most men have. How am I going to satisfy her?"

"I'm afraid I'll never be able to reach a climax. I'll die of embarrassment."

"I'm not big like a lot of guys."

The more we stew about it, the more apprehensive we become. Sometimes we're almost immobilized by feelings of inadequacy.

Another strong deterrent to our sexual enjoyment is the

issue of morality. Even though we're adults and allowed to do all the things we couldn't wait to do "when we grow up," we're often stuck with the beliefs we formed as children. Many of the thoughts that plague us now are the result of attitudes our parents instilled in us for our protection or our own good.

We still have little tape players in our minds. They play endless tapes of old "shoulds" and "shouldn'ts" that influence our behavior and feelings, even when we're not aware of it. Complicating the problem is the fact that every one of us has different tapes. Yet most of us think our own beliefs are the "right" ones.

Women born in the 1930s knew zilch about sex. Our mothers blushed at the very mention of the word and could hardly explain the physical process to us, let alone the emotional dynamics. As little girls, we quickly learned our parts "down there" were not to be touched or looked at. My own mother tried hard not to overreact when she saw Betty and me "playing nurse" behind the oleanders. But her very manner and expression as she called us in for cookies indicated great discomfort and shame. When I copied my brother's phrase, "They caught me with my pants down," my mother called me aside and told me quietly it wasn't a nice thing for a girl to say.

We grew up filled with doubts about the appropriateness of our sexuality. Each of us had to struggle with making our own codes and beliefs just as much as older women, though perhaps in different ways.

One moral code everybody agrees on, though, is that sex between husband and wife is perfectly appropriate and desirable, and is to be enjoyed. It seems we shouldn't have problems in that area, yet we do.

"He'd like oral sex and I think it's wrong."

"I'm ashamed I have fantasies about other men while

I'm having intercourse with my husband."

"I feel guilty about using birth control because of my religion, so I never really enjoy sex."

"Even though I know it's all right now that I'm married, I still somehow feel dirty doing it."

"Sex with girl friends and prostitutes is one thing. But I feel like my wife is so good and pure I can't get turned on to her."

"I'm so dependent on my husband, he feels like a father figure. It seems incestuous to make love with him."

How do we deal with these moral dilemmas? Communication. We need to talk to our mates and express our fears, doubts and concerns. We can consult many other sources for education and reassurance—our priests, ministers, rabbis, marriage counselors. Even books on the subject help us make our decisions.

In the end, making decisions is up to us. We can draw on all kinds of sources, but we have to decide for ourselves what we believe is right and wrong.

Once we determine what we believe, we have to *do* it—or *not* do it, as the case may be. Changing our beliefs doesn't automatically change our feelings in a jiffy. It takes time to get used to new beliefs and feelings.

If I decide I want to turn over a new leaf and become wildly erotic, experimenting with all sorts of sexual play, I have to give myself permission first. Then I have to plunge in and try it, even if I feel embarrassed and uncomfortable. Only by *doing* it will my feelings begin to change. Soon I may find myself really enjoying all the new behavior, but I won't ever enjoy it unless I start.

New feelings and behavior have to come from our own decision that we *want* to change, and that we believe it's OK. If someone else is trying to get me to change while I truly believe such behavior is wrong, I'll probably never enjoy it. It just won't work.

What do we do in a case like that? If one person in the marriage thinks oral sex is terrific and the other thinks it's dreadful, all we can do is approach the problem like any other problem. Try compromise and negotiation along with communication. "I'm willing to try oral sex if you'll paint the porch." Or "Gee, honey, in spite of all the books that encourage it and even though Father Doyle says it's fine, I still can't bring myself to do it. I'm really sorry . . . I guess we'll never be perfectly matched in every way, will we? But remember, even the worst sex is terrific!"

There are other problems in our sexual endeavors that may seem relatively unimportant. But they can be disheartening nonetheless.

"I'm a night person; he's a morning person. He falls asleep even before I get my teeth brushed, so we never get to make love at night. Then in the morning, he's grabbing for my parts while I'm still sound asleep. I get upset with him."

Solution? Compromise. "We make love two nights a week and two mornings a week." Or "This week we do it at night. Next week we do it mornings." That's fair and respectful.

"Sex is boring. Always exactly the same." Sonia and Tim made up fantasies to tell each other and acted out the ones that were feasible. Tina and Chuck tried a few X-rated movies. Molly and Michael bought books on variation and technique. Boring sex is easy to liven up when both parties are willing to experiment.

Another common complaint is, "I'm so afraid of getting pregnant I can't relax." That's a very real problem and one I won't try to solve. All you can do is investigate the different kinds of birth control that are available and find which is best for you. Take solace in the fact you'll eventually be past menopause. You'll never have to worry again. There *are* some advantages to age!

"I'm so aware of the kids. I hear every little sound. I can't relax and enjoy sex when one of them is crying or calling for me."

That's a tough one. Generally, mothers are more in tune with their children's sounds because they spend more time taking care of them. It's difficult to turn off a feeling of responsibility. It's harder to let ourselves get into a sexual experience when we hear a child crying.

Here we need to consider frequency. If children are in the habit of crying or yelling for you often at night, you need to change your response pattern. If a child is in genuine need, you'll probably have to shatter the loving mood and go tend to him. Hopefully you can get the loving feelings back afterward.

I encourage parents to start closing their bedroom doors when their children are very young. You'll still be able to hear them if they cry or call out in need. But they'll grow up with the knowledge that parents enjoy privacy. Most parents leave the door open so they'll be able to hear what's going on. This can cause problems when the kids get older.

Mary Lou said, "As soon as Jim and I close the door to our bedroom, the kids gather right outside in the hall. They ask for snacks and wonder what we're doing. We can't relax with that going on!"

Indeed, they can't. Children should learn at an early age that parents need to be alone. But if you can't bring yourself to close your door all night every night, close yourselves in for short periods on a regular basis. Leave orders you're not to be disturbed unless it's an emergency. You don't have to make love every time, but you get the kids used to your privacy together so it will be accepted and taken for granted.

It's also good modeling for them. They'll know *they* deserve privacy when they're grown up and married.

The most common problem I encounter is the variance in sexual appetites. The best solution is compromise. One couple who solved it beautifully were Janet and Vince.

Janet had a fairly low sex drive, while Vince seemed to think about nothing else. When I asked how often they thought they'd like sex if it were up to them, Janet piped up, "Once a month," just as Vince was saying, "Three times a day!"

What they did was find a number in between the two extremes. It took a lot of communication and discussion. Their reasoning was so skilled it would have made any debate team sit up and take notice. But they finally settled on "every four days."

It was considerably more often than Janet would have liked. But the agreement included the fact she could lie there and think about anything she wanted during the process because Vince was the one who "needed" sex. Because they really loved each other and wanted to cooperate, the solution was fine.

Another couple had the same problem in reverse. Jennifer was the physically affectionate one. Bill was relatively disinterested. In their case, we added manual stimulation, a vibrator. Jennifer was the one who wanted orgasm frequently, so she was delighted to have him apply the vibrator. In no time at all she reached a climax. Granted, it wasn't the proverbial "web of ecstasy," but it was satisfying nonetheless. Bill agreed he would satisfy Jennifer twice a week by whatever means he chose. He used the vibrator when he didn't feel like getting more involved himself.

Some people object to compromise and negotiation in

sex on the grounds it takes the joy and spontaneity out of romance. It makes sex a business agreement instead of an act of love. But those who are willing to try it generally find it solves their problems. As I said before, once we get involved, we often find ourselves turning on after all.

Although sex is important, it is *not* the most important thing in marriage. Sometimes we get so focused on our Sexual Problems we lose sight of all the good things we have going for us. If you can take the pressure off by using some of these suggestions, do it. But recognize that sex alone doesn't determine the quality of a relationship.

I know many couples who deeply love each other. The joy they find in being together is beautiful to see. They have common interests, mutual respect and senses of humor that keep the marriage well nourished. They have varying degrees of sexual incompatibility, but they accept those the way people accept any other problems in life. They make the best of the good things they have going for them.

I've known other couples who had superb sex lives. They enjoyed sex all the way to the divorce court because there wasn't much else in their relationship.

I don't know of any couple who has a perfect sex life. We all have problems in that area. So if you have sex problems, isn't it nice to know you're normal? Relax and join the club.

A final note: A book on marriage would be incomplete without a chapter devoted to sex. As I began to write this chapter, I found myself wanting to say virtually the same things I already said in my first book, *Out Of Apples?* So, you're right if you think what you just read sounded familiar. I decided to use the original chapter in case you hadn't had a chance to read *Out of Apples?* And even if you have, it never hurts to brush up on sex!

Forsaking All Others

All others?

How many others?

Exactly how much do we have to forsake? That's a question we practically never think of before the wedding, because we can't imagine ever wanting to spend time with anyone but our beloved spouse-to-be. But in most marriages, the question arises sooner or later, because we're human.

Human beings have the capacity to love more than one person. Our children are good examples. We're sometimes surprised at how much we love each child, each in a little different way. They all have qualities and traits that differ from the others, and we value them for their differences as well as their similarities.

Our dear friend Bill McCartin used to say, "Love is not like jam, of which there's only so much to put on toast. Love is endless. We can love many people in many ways."

Perhaps that's both a blessing and a curse. It's fantastic to enjoy loving people. Sometimes it's catastrophic as well. But the problem isn't love; it's what we *do* with the love.

Ideally we'd determine our beliefs about fidelity and make sure we agree before we get to the altar. Probably most of us *assume* both parties will be faithful. Some couples do discuss the issue and are easily able to promise fidelity, because in that state of euphoria they can't imagine being attracted to anyone else.

In some marriages the problem never arises. Often couples who share a strong religious bond keep themselves on the straight and narrow with never a thought of going astray. That's also true of many people without the spiritual backbone, who have a lot of integrity and would never allow themselves to do anything that goes against their moral or ethical values.

At the other end of the spectrum are couples whose relationships are fraught with extramarital affairs that bring a lot of pain to one or both people involved, as well as to the "other person."

There are all kinds of variations in between. I know many couples with agreements vastly different from Larry's and mine, who are living happily together. If what they do works for them, I can only applaud them, whether or not it matches my value system.

Years ago we met a couple that both of us immediately liked. They were pillars of the church, always heading up various committees and activities, as well as being excellent parents. And they were fun to be with. As we got to know them better we learned a surprising fact: Both of them had continual affairs. They had been married some 20 years by then, and had agreed from the start that one lover apiece would never be enough; they both preferred a variety. With that agreement they got married and have managed to continue that lifestyle ever since. They're still together, still happy, and still having affairs outside the marriage.

Unusual? For sure. How can it work? They agree and they're honest. There is no deceit going on. She'll announce at dinner, "I'll be spending Tuesday afternoons with my new boyfriend, so I won't be cooking those days."

He will nod agreeably and be happy for her, because he is enjoying Wednesday evenings with his girlfriend.

When they told us about their arrangement we were more than a little incredulous, and I felt like a child learning the facts of life. I kept saying, "You *do?* He *does?* She *is?*" and feeling very naive that such a situation could be happening.

They went on to explain that they'd had to experiment a bit to work things out properly. They'd begun by being so honest they even told each other who the other parties were, but discovered that caused some discomfort when they found themselves at the same social gatherings. So they discussed it some more and decided to keep names out of it, but continue telling each other when something was going on.

Now, please don't get the impression that I'm recommending this! My misgivings about the whole situation include the obvious dangers like AIDS, as well as the ethics and morals concerning the other partners, what happens to them and their spouses, and all kinds of potential pain that I see as inevitable. I still find it totally amazing that it's worked between these two people, but they want it to work and have made it happen.

Completely opposite from these people would be the couple who agree on no contact whatsoever with anyone of the opposite sex. One man I know refuses to let his wife go to the obstetrician alone. He insists on being there for each examination during her pregnancies as well as the actual birth. She must let no man into their home unless he's there, not even his brothers. He has a lot more freedom than she, incidentally, but both of them find that arrangement acceptable.

They seem as happy as the couple with the multiple sex partners.

It's not our job to judge any of these people and their choices. We need to focus our energies on deciding what we believe is fair and comfortable for ourselves.

Most folks, I think, agree that a husband and wife should be faithful to each other, and I think more couples honor that agreement than dishonor it. Certainly there is a lot of cheating in the world, but by and large it's not condoned by either the cheaters or the cheatees.

"It just happened; we didn't intend for it to happen," is a defense I hear quite a lot. Most of the time it goes against people's moral values to have an affair. Still, there are many individuals who truly believe an affair is acceptable if it happens out of town.

I have heard men and women alike confess to exciting rendezvous while they're away on business trips. Many of them subscribe to the adage, "What you don't know won't hurt you."

My opinion? It *will* hurt you. I personally believe that we can't beat the system.

I remember fondly one particular client who was most unsatisfied with a marriage that was practically sexless. Her husband spent most of his free time playing golf; the rest of it masturbating with magazines. His wife, whom I'll call Nancy, was frustrated and discouraged. She came in for counseling even though her husband refused.

Nancy was a travel agent and earned an all-expense-paid trip to Bermuda. When she got home, she came in for her appointment and was high as a kite on excitement and adventure. It was fun to see her so glowing, but I was concerned when she told me about the Australian she'd picked up in a bar and taken home to sleep with.

"Nancy, that scares me to death," I said. "You didn't even know him. What if he had herpes or something?" (This was in the days before AIDS.)

Nancy shrugged with unconcern and said, "No problem; I already have herpes."

So that's great. Now the Australian might have been taking herpes home to his unsuspecting wife.

Most of us try at some time to beat the system and go against the rules, and sometimes we get away with it. At least we don't always get caught. But in a larger sense, going against the rules does some damage to our self-esteem and our trust in other people.

The most paranoid people in the world are the cheaters. They don't trust *anybody!* Their attitude of distrust builds walls around themselves, keeping any kind of deep emotional relationship at arm's length. They look askance at people who maintain their innocence because they *know* people lie and cheat.

What is cheating? An "affair" may mean different things to different people. In the old movie *An Affair To Remember,* two people fall in love and decide to marry but are kept apart for years by a tragic accident. Eventually they reunite and all is understood. It was a wonderful love story set in the 1950s, and there was no indication of physical sex between them. In those days a love affair was usually the process of falling in love and/or being in love. Most of the time it led to marriage, and *that* is when the sex happened.

But that was the "olden days." Today most people assume an affair includes sexual intercourse, so for now we'll use that definition.

Most of us would not condone or tolerate a spouse's

cheating, and yet it seems to be a frequently occurring behavior. Certainly it's often discussed in marriage counselors' offices.

There seems to be a fairly common process involved.
Typically the parties involved did not plan to have the affair. If I combined stories of the last 30 people who discussed the subject with me I would come up with the
following recitation. (I'll write it as if it's a woman talking,
but it could just as easily be a man. Certainly it takes one
of each to make it happen!)

"We never meant for this to happen. I've worked in the
same office with Don for four years. We've always been
friends, but there was never anything more between us.
We know each other's husband and wife, and we like
each other. That's probably what troubles me more than
anything else right now, knowing I'm hurting two people
I really care about.

"I'm miserable. I've lost 14 pounds, I can't sleep, I can't
eat, and I have a constant knot in my stomach. Sometimes
I just wish I could get in the car and drive out of town;
maybe go to California and start a new life with a new
name and everything, but I couldn't because I love my
kids too much.

"Can you love two men? I honestly do love my
husband, and I love Don, too. But the love I feel for my
husband is not nearly as exciting. I mean I *care* about him
and don't want to hurt him, but with Don it's thrilling to
be in the same room. Sometimes I wonder if I ever did
love my husband, or if we just got married because it was
the thing to do. I don't remember ever feeling this way
toward him.

"But the kids would just die if we got a divorce. The
other night one of them asked me if Daddy and I would
ever get divorced and I almost threw up. Don doesn't

want a divorce either because of his children.

"There is no way I can resolve this situation without feeling a tremendous amount of pain. Whatever way I go is unbearable. I can't give Don up, but neither can I leave my husband and hurt the kids so much. They adore their daddy."

I feel so much compassion for clients who are telling me this because they are clearly suffering. It is truly a no-win situation, with inevitable pain. It is listening to this pain so many times that makes me say, "It isn't worth it. You can't beat the system."

Naturally, I never say that to the person who is admitting this problem. He or she already knows it. I only say it *before* the fact if I get a chance.

One of my favorite movies is *A Touch of Class,* in which George Segal and Glenda Jackson play the parts of two strangers who start out with the intention of "a little good sex" and end up terribly in love and finally devastated at having to end the affair because he's married to someone else. It's a brilliantly acted comedy, but the end always makes me cry. I recommend it to anyone considering an affair.

Affairs almost always cause more pain than pleasure. But there are a thousand rationalizations for having them. It all boils down to one belief: I am entitled to have what I want.

I am every bit as susceptible to that mistaken belief as anyone else . . . I often convince myself I deserve what I want. Fortunately or unfortunately, the price I would have to pay usually jogs my better judgment. But not always. If I had thought about it yesterday, I wouldn't have pigged out at the Sunday brunch birthday party. This morning I groaned at the scale, announced it was time for severe self-deprivation and discipline, and went out for a brisk walk to prove I meant business. Regretful as I felt, though, I hurt nobody but myself.

With affairs it's different. Somebody else almost always gets hurt.

One of the most common excuses I hear is, "If my marriage were good in the first place I wouldn't have been susceptible to falling in love with someone else."

Maybe so. But practically all of us have marriages so "bad" from time to time that we're vulnerable. Certainly it's tempting to run into the arms of the nearest attractive person, but it doesn't solve anything. It's like having your car battery die and leaving the car to go steal someone else's. We would never do that; we'd get the battery recharged to put our own car back in working condition.

But that's logical reasoning, and falling in love is totally illogical. The feelings are overwhelming, no matter who we're falling in love with.

I use the word "overwhelming" with some caution, however, because I think it almost gives us permission to do what we feel like doing. To be overwhelmed is to be helpless in the face of temptation, or whatever feeling is taking over. In truth I don't think we are ever out of control unless we let ourselves be.

I wish I had a nickel for every time I've developed a crush on another man. I fall in love very easily! So do lots of other people. But we all have the capacity to choose our behavior based on what will be best for us in the long run.

Another common excuse for affairs is simply boredom. Most of us like a certain level of excitement in our lives, and when it's missing we look to fill it up with something. Few things are as exciting as affairs.

But few things are as exciting as hang gliding, either, or parachute jumping, and most of us don't get involved in those activities.

Having an affair is an easy high. How can anything that feels so good and is so easy to come by be resisted? Admittedly, sometimes it takes all the willpower we can conjure up. It's not easy. Staying faithful may be one of the biggest challenges we face.

We're so capable of convincing ourselves that it's okay to do whatever we feel like doing, that it's tough to convince ourselves it's *not* all right. Recently I heard someone say, "The greatest pain is caused by trying to hold onto the greatest pleasure."

This seems to ring true with affairs. The thrilling sensations and the excitement of forbidden fruit are almost too good to pass up. Those feelings are the greatest pleasures. We'd be crazy not to want them! But they do seem to cause the greatest pain. To avoid the pain you must forego the pleasure.

Nobody said we get to have everything we want in life. Still, we can enjoy wanting whatever it is. Feelings are never right or wrong; only our behavior is.

Every morning I dutifully walk a brisk 30 or 40 minutes, and my favorite route takes me to a nearby shopping center. You know why? Because there's a cinnamon-roll shop there that makes cinnamon rolls good enough to die for! I can sniff the scent in the air when I get close to the building, and it gets more and more enticing the closer I get to the shop. Finally, I walk right in front of it. I get to look in the windows and watch them rolling the dough and putting pats of butter along the strips, sprinkling them with cinnamon and sugar, and popping the pans into the oven. People are always inside eating rolls with their coffee and I glance at them with envy, but I continue walking. I do not go in, even though my heart and soul are there! Why don't I treat myself to a cinnamon roll? Because it would be bad for me. They must have a thousand calories each, and it wouldn't be worth the pain I'd feel as I got fatter and fatter . . . which is what would happen if I didn't discipline myself to avoid them.

So, in the long run, I'm happier not eating rolls than I would be eating them. I've eaten enough in my life to know the feelings of guilt and regret, and I don't need those.

For me it's more positive to walk on by than to succumb. It's the same with men. They're sweet and spicy, and tantalizing and inviting, too, and I enjoy them with almost as much enthusiasm and gusto as I do cinnamon rolls. (Well, not *quite* so much.) But they're not for me to enjoy at a physical level. I don't need the pain.

Sometimes we lean toward affairs in order to see if we've "still got it." Maybe we want to test our power and make sure we're still attractive to the opposite sex. Goodness knows we can look like death sometimes when we get up on an ordinary morning. In fact I once heard a sermon that recommended this strategy to anyone whose spouse indulged in an affair: "Take a picture of your husband or wife first thing in the morning and mail it to the lover."

Certainly that would be the end of *my* affair, if I were to have one. I know my husband loves me if only because he's seen me in my faded flannel nightgown a million times and still calls me "Cutie!"

He and I laugh sometimes when we're all dressed up to go someplace, and we look at each other and say, "This is the *real* us!" We laugh because it is definitely *not* the real us. What is? Old worn nightclothes, soft old jeans, comfortable sweatshirts and sneakers.

Comfort is wonderful. And yet it's the very thing that makes us hunger for excitement.

For me, the answer is friendship with men. It's the best of both worlds. I can revel in the comfort I feel with Larry. I don't have to act scintillating and/or look gorgeous and be sparkling. I'm free to be the real me in all my faded old clothes, and so is he. What a lovely freedom that is; not to have to impress.

On the other hand, it's fun to impress sometimes, both Larry and other people. I delight in getting dressed up and being sparkling. I like to be a little flirtatious. I like to turn on and feel attractive. It's fun to laugh and learn new things about new people. People are there for us to enjoy! God forbid that I ever take cinnamon rolls so for granted that I don't drink in the sight and scent when I walk by. God forbid, too, that I ever turn off the part of myself that notices and appreciates men.

But God forbid that I ever have an affair. It would spoil so many things. For one thing, I couldn't feel the confidence I now have to enjoy men without feeling any apprehension.

If I felt I couldn't trust myself with another man, it would put a damper on any friendship I might have with one. Knowing I'm firmly in charge of my behavior frees me to have lunch with men friends as comfortably as I do with women friends.

"But why do you need to have lunch with men?" asked a client who was objecting to his wife's desire to do the same thing. "It only puts you in a dangerous position that you might not be strong enough to get out of. Why risk? Don't let yourself be tempted."

He has a point. There would be no alcoholics if people never took a drink. I don't think for a minute that people should drink if they prefer not drinking. By the same token they shouldn't have friends of the opposite sex if they doubt their ability to resist more than friendship.

Each of us must make those decisions for ourselves.

But to answer the man's question, "Why risk it?" I would say this: Men and women are different in so many ways. What a shame it is to rule out half the human race just because they're the wrong sex. We learn and grow from spending time with people, and the more people we see the more pleasure we enjoy.

Many of us are content enjoying the awareness of another person's general sexuality, without having to get involved with genital sexuality. The latter is what gets us in trouble.

Why do I like men? They have interesting appearances. I like looking at them. They often have good senses of humor, and I love to laugh. They have different perspectives on a lot of subjects, and can be fun to argue with.

Why does Larry enjoy women? I asked him. "They have different viewpoints," he said after a moment's thought. "And having lunch with another woman gives me a chance to feel admired. Other women are not as honest with me as you are, so there's usually no criticism or negativity over lunch. That's nice."

I admit I blanched for a second at his answer. What, *me* . . . critical and negative? But I must plead guilty. My expectations of him are probably more intense than they are for any other person in the world and, therefore, so are my disappointments. And, furthermore, I verbalize them freely to him.

As he does with me.

Some would say therein lies the danger of man/woman friendships; that surface kind of non-threatening conversation can be so refreshing that it makes us hungry for more. It's such fun to act like we're wonderfully easy to get along with, when those we live with know we're really not.

When I have lunch with a man, I can listen with interest to new stories and jokes. (Larry and I have few *new* stories to share after 36 years.) I can overlook the too-strong cologne on a man I'll talk to for only an hour; I can't handle the pungency on someone with whom I share my life so intimately. So Larry hears me complain immediately and vociferously about any infraction of his that threatens my sense of comfort. Wayne doesn't. Right or wrong, I can afford to be a little kinder to Wayne, Fred or Frank because I leave them promptly after lunch. They don't *have* to know my feelings and thoughts on so intimate and honest a level.

On the other hand, they don't *get* to know. To me the intimate, honest sharing is a precious gift, though admittedly it rankles sometimes. If it's true that we can have as good a relationship with someone as we are honest with them, my relationship with Larry is bound to be a million times better than most just because of its honesty.

But it sure is fun to have a drink with Eddie after work now and then. Eddie sees me only as warm, fun and happy. He's never seen the bitchy side of me. He doesn't know how picky I am when we look for motels on vacations. Larry could tell him how frustrating it is to hear me reject this motel because the room smells like cigars, and that one because the train goes right behind it, and the other one because it's under the flight pattern. By the time we find the perfect motel Larry sighs, "Praise the Lord," and wonders why he chose *me*.

Eddie will always see me only as "easy to please." I have an image to uphold with him, and it's easy because our visits are so few and far between. I've no doubt that if Eddie and I were married, both of us would see entirely different people in each other than we see now. Of course it's fun to have a drink with him after work now and then;

I get to act like I'm a joy to be with. That's how Larry gets to act over lunch with Nancy, Kathy, Rosemary or any of the other women he enjoys seeing.

As long as we're able to keep the opposite-sex relationships on purely a friendship level, there is no problem. What happens if we don't? Then we complicate our lives badly, as well as the lives of the other man or woman.

There was a man, many years ago, who was a close friend of the whole family. He was single, so he had lots of friends all over town, and he was a very loving person. Everyone who knew him loved him. Larry and I shared our problems with him as well as just doing things together that were fun. Both of us treasured him.

One day when he and I were chatting about love and marriage and commitments he said something to me that I've never forgotten.

"Lee, you know how much I like you. I love you. There are times that I'd like to go to bed with you, but it would spoil everything."

"I know," I responded, and neither of us said anything more. Shortly after that he moved away, but I've always been so glad he said what he did. I delight in the memory of his warmth and honesty and affection. I even quote him now and then when people are considering having an affair. I, too, believe it would "spoil everything."

A married person can't cross that line from friendship and affection to sexual love without paying an enormous price. But there's nothing wrong with telling another person how you feel about him or her, as long as it doesn't lead to the next level of intimacy.

Some people are unable to stop there. I have a good friend I'll call Kate. She's divorced and has had a couple of affairs with married men, which she now regrets. Kate confided to me that she no longer trusts herself when it comes to keeping a friendship simply a friendship.

"I can't afford to put myself in that vulnerable position again," she said. "I can have lunch with a married man if it's business or if it includes his wife, but I can't have the luxury of situations that might lead to romance."

She's probably very wise. Her track record is not a good one when it comes to backing away from married men. I have a lot of respect for her new intentions and I have no doubt she'll stick to them. She knows herself well . . . now.

"I still don't trust myself," Kate explains. "You don't get rid of addictions. You just learn to control them."

Is sex an addiction? There is a lot of conjuring about that question these days. Some people scoff angrily and say, "That's just a way to allow yourself to have affairs and not feel guilty. It's a cop out."

I agree that mankind has always found ways to excuse bad behavior. My friend John claims his affairs are "because I'm an Aries. Aries always have affairs." Some men attribute their wanderings to their fathers, who taught them, "It's what men have to do. In Europe everybody has mistresses." People can always rationalize. "I require a lot of sex and my wife doesn't. It's a kindness to her that I go elsewhere for part of it."

While having affairs used to be more of a masculine trait, today's women are much less restrained than they used to be. I know a lot of married women who have cheated on their husbands and used variations on the same reasoning.

"I needed to find out what sex is like with other men. I was a virgin when I married, and I had to know how other men did it."

"Life was no fun anymore. It was either have an affair or a nervous breakdown. I think it kept me from getting a divorce."

And the classic, "I didn't mean for it to happen. It just did." (It's not my fault because I didn't plan it.)

Since time began people have had sex with people when they weren't supposed to, but it's only recently that sex has been considered by some to be an addiction. There is no chemical dependency like there is in alcohol or drug abuse. But the alleged addiction stems from the temporary high one feels in the challenge, the chase and the triumph. The feeling of self-esteem comes strongly to those people when they've made another conquest.

If we define addiction as a habit that we can't seem to break in spite of the pain it causes ourselves and/or others, then sex would surely qualify. Many people have ruined their lives because of it, losing their spouses and families, and yet they continue down this path of destruction because of a burning "need" to prove themselves worthwhile.

Since we've already talked about the word "need," you know I don't believe it's a need at all, but rather a strong want. Either way it's a big motivator.

Addictions can also be positive. Dr. William Glasser says in his book *Positive Addictions*[1] that it's good to have an interest that is so rewarding it becomes almost consuming. Doing that particular activity restores us in some way, feeds us and rejuvenates us. We feel a sense of loss when we can't pursue that activity. Runners may feel let down if weather or illness prevents them from running. Artists feel they "need" to paint, and musicians look for bands in which they can "sit in" even when they're on vacation.

Perhaps any activity itself isn't good or bad, but our use of it can be. I saw a marriage break up over tennis, a sport we think of as healthy activity. The husband was so driven by his desire to improve his tennis game that it took precedence over everything else in his life, including his wife.

I believe almost anything can become an addiction. So I'm not uncomfortable with the term "sexual addiction" any more than I would be with "mudpie addiction."

The important thing is what we do about it. I applaud anyone who looks for ways to get back in control of his or her life. The 12-step program that has been used to help millions of alcoholics, drug addicts, gamblers and overeaters has been extremely successful. I can't recommend it enough to people with problems.

The Twelve Steps

1. We admit we are powerless over compulsive sexual behavior and that our lives had become unmanageable.

2. Come to believe that a Power greater than ourselves could restore us to sanity.

3. Make a decision to turn our will and our lives over to the care of God as we understand him. Combat the isolation we feel and belief that we alone have to solve our problems.

4. Make a searching and fearless moral inventory.

5. Admit to God, to ourselves and to another person the exact nature of our wrongs.

6. We are entirely ready to have God remove all these defects of character.

7. Humbly ask him to remove our shortcomings.

8. Make a list of all persons you have harmed, and become willing to make amends to them all.

9. Make direct amends to such people wherever possible, except when to do so would injure them or others.

10. Continue to take personal inventory, and when we are wrong, promptly admit it.

11. Seek through prayer and meditation to improve our conscious contact with God as we understand him, praying for knowledge of His will for us and the power to carry it out.

12. Carry the message of recovery to other people in need, and to live our own lives according to the principles of The Steps.

Daily recitation of the Serenity Prayer reminds us how to live our lives according to the twelve steps: "God grant me the serenity to accept the things I cannot change, courage to change the things I can, and wisdom to know the difference."

Those who feel they are addicted have found a sense of relief at finding a group of supporters who truly understand and share the problem. If you're struggling with the pain that comes from having a spouse who cheats on you, or if you're dealing with the pain that comes from cheating, I suggest you write to the National Association on Sexual Addiction Problems, Inc., and find a local chapter.

Also, one of my friends has just written a book that deals with sexual addictions. I suggest it to you for in-depth information by a professional who has had first-hand experience with a sexual addict she loves very much . . . and he her. Together they've discovered Sex Anonymous and found it most helpful in understanding what they're trying to deal with. The book is titled *Back from Betrayal.* [2]

Addiction or otherwise, the consensus is that affairs don't make anybody happy for long. They'll continue to tantalize us, appeal to us and sometimes seduce us, but they won't be the source of lasting happiness.

That's not new information, of course. Almost all of us were taught that message by our Sunday school teachers, priests, ministers, rabbis and parents. I used to think "sin" was forbidden because God said so, and that God sat up there watching to see if we did something evil so he could zap punishment on us.

Now, I've come to believe that all the moral laws and ethical values we were taught over the years have been suggested not only by religious leaders, but by ordinary people like you and me, who have tried these things and found them to cause pain. My friend Kendra McNally defines sin as "anything that's bad for me."

Sometimes it seems like we have to try out behavior for ourselves to see what the results will be. It's too bad we can't learn everything in life just by listening to or reading information handed down by "experts," but we don't. We keep reinventing the wheel, rediscovering that "If I do this it's going to cause pain to somebody, including me." We keep taking risks and learning for ourselves what we can and can't get away with. In a larger sense that's probably good.

How do we handle the hurt, though, that comes when someone we love is still experimenting with other people? Can we forgive infidelity? That deserves a chapter to itself.

1. William Glasser, *Positive Addiction,* New York, Harper & Row, 1985.
2. Dr. Jennifer Schneider, *Back from Betrayal,* New York , Harper & Row, 1988.

Chapter 10

Forgiving

If I'd realized *why* I should do it, I might have forgiven people all along! Like so many of those other early teachings, "You must forgive one another" fell on my relatively deaf ears, except to make me mildly uncomfortable when I thought of all the people I didn't want to forgive.

I went for a whole year without speaking to my closest friend, Marie Magee, when we were in junior high. We walked the exact same path twice daily, nine blocks to and from school, on opposite sides of the street without acknowledging each other's presence. I really missed her, too, but I wouldn't consider forgiving her.

One day my mother called her over and "introduced" us and we giggled. We were friends again. Still, I never consciously "forgave" her. (Marie, if you read this, I forgive you. I just can't remember what I'm forgiving you for!)

Forgiving is one of the most difficult things to do. If we're hurt by someone, we have a tendency to keep that hurt alive and close to our hearts, even though it damages our relationship dramatically. Fanning the fire of hurt takes a lot of remembering, but we're good rememberers.

Especially women.

Men are better at forgiving because they forget. Women forget very little, so we have a harder time forgiving.

But men and women alike can hang onto old hurts tenaciously, almost cherishing them. Some of us get them out and look at them frequently, like we do photo albums, keeping alive the pain we felt when Uncle Jerry ate our chocolate bunny when we were four years old, or whatever. Boy oh boy, we muse; that hurt! And can you believe Donna took away my date and kissed him at midnight at the New Year's Eve party? That was in 1949, and I remember it like it was yesterday. And in 1952, Mrs. White accused me of stealing stamps from the dormitory desk. Sure did hurt my feelings. In 1957 Larry called his folks but not mine when our second baby was born.

This is all from the woman who can't remember dates from history. Wars are unimportant, but my personal hurts? We're talking earthshakingly major!

I hate to admit it, but I'll bet I could jot down a lengthy list of remembered injustices that I have endured lo these many years. Have I forgiven them all? I like to think so, but the fact that I remember them so well makes me wonder.

But it's only been in the past few years that I've realized that forgiveness is for the forgiver's benefit rather than the forgivee's. Life is miserable for the hater. Have you ever been so angry with someone that you stiffened at the sight of his car or mention of his name? Your pleasant mood was absolutely ruined if that person happened onto the scene. And he could say nothing that didn't make you furious. I've experienced only one person like that, and that's all anyone needs in a lifetime.

If he said, "It might rain today," it made me livid. I'm

chagrined to admit the loathing I felt for him, and I felt totally helpless to change the situation. So I carried my evil secret around for years. Guess who was the miserable one? He appeared to be quite happy, actually, and that made me even madder. That one relationship taught me how hard it is to maintain an angry, resentful feeling for someone and endure the relentless discomfort that goes with hating.

In my defense, I was young. I like to think I've learned a lot since then. If faced with that same situation today, I'd have at least a dozen options I could pursue to resolve the problem. For starters I'd simply tell him my feelings; the good old "When you . . . I feel . . . because . . . ."

In those days I didn't know I had that right, so I kept the feelings deep inside me. Generally that's what causes hate—at least it encourages the process. The more we keep bottled up, the more hostile we feel, until we're like balloons ready to pop. It's a miserable feeling, and one we've all experienced.

My daughter Lisa says, "Our lives are shaped by those who love us and those who refuse to love us."

It's probably good for us to have folks around who refuse to love us because it calls on us to learn to cope. Naturally, we'd rather be surrounded by those who love us and believe in us and encourage us, and hopefully we have some of those. But we also learn a lot from the others. We can get tougher by being exposed to the tough people. We can come to terms with the fact that there are some people who simply will never like us, let alone love us, and we can stand that.

I've heard that one person out of ten will not like me. (Or you either.) So when someone shows signs of dislike we can tell ourselves happily, "Oh good, that's the one out of ten . . . the next nine will, no doubt, think I'm delightful!"

Life is not easy. Some people dislike us. They hurt us, they reject us, and we suffer. No matter that *they* might be terribly unhappy themselves; look what they do to *us*.

Much of our unhappiness comes from being treated unfairly (in our eyes) by inconsiderate, insensitive or just downright mean people. You may have seen the bumper sticker, "Hell is other people." Each of us has our deeply imbedded set of "shoulds" about the way folks ought to treat each other, and they're constantly being violated. And yet most of us truly believe *we* are not the bad guys . . . *they* are.

Many times I have this experience in my counseling office. A woman comes in and describes her pain at living with a man who sounds totally uncaring. Often she cries as she talks. She doubts that anything will ever change in their relationship because this man thinks *she's* the one with the problem, and he's not about to conform to her wishes. She's desperate, angry and depressed. As I listen, I have to agree that it would be tough living with that set of circumstances; and that if I were her, I'd feel as bad as she does. I empathize with her heartache and strongly urge that she ask her husband to come in, too.

"It would be so much more efficient," I explain. "If all three of us can get together, we can solve things more quickly than if you're the only one coming for counseling. Perhaps he'd come in for a session by himself so he could tell me how he sees things."

The fascinating thing is this: When he does come in, he turns out to be a good guy, too. As I listen to his view of the relationship, I hear the pain *he's* been experiencing. It's been rotten for him, as well. He's disappointed and demoralized and thoroughly discouraged; afraid to hope things will ever change because she's so sure she's right and he's wrong. He doesn't see it that way.

I feel the same understanding and compassion for him that I did for her, and agree with a lot of what he says. The next step is for them to come together.

Often they've compared notes before they come back, and are surprised to discover that I sympathized with them both. I accepted them both; even *liked* them both! Once in a while they're a bit hostile, each one hurt that I didn't find the other one to be wrong, faulty, flawed . . . the bad guy, the cause of the problem.

Truly, I've never met a "bad guy" yet. Often someone *sounds* bad when I hear the other's description, but later they make good sense when they explain their views.

I am convinced that most of us are good. We do not want to be mean or inconsiderate. We went into marriage in good faith, with every intention of loving this person forever and being a good spouse.

But that doesn't take away the hurt we've suffered living with a mate who sees things so differently.

What needs to happen somewhere down the road is *forgiveness*.

Until I can forgive the person who's hurt me I'm going to feel discomfort. When I say that to a client I often see a setting of the jaw and a steely anger in the eyes. "Forgive?" they say incredulously. "I can *never* forgive. This person has hurt me too many times."

I understand. It may be way too soon to even consider forgiveness, and there's no rush. But gently I go on to talk about it as an eventual goal *for their own sake,* not the other person's.

When we're able to forgive, we feel immediate relief. The letting-go is dramatic. It's like a magic pill that makes a headache disappear instantly. It has a much greater impact on the forgiver than it ever can on the forgivee. Once again we're lightened; free to resume living without this giant burden weighing us down. And we did it all by ourselves!

It may have very little to do with the other person. He or she may not even know we've forgiven them. But *we* know, and that makes all the difference.

What holds us back, then? If forgiveness feels so all-fired great, why is it so hard to do?

Probably because we're scared. If we forgive, we might leave ourselves vulnerable again. As it is now, we've built this wall of resentment around ourselves, which we think keeps us safe from hurt. If we don't let other people get close anymore, we'll stay secure. Forgiveness would take away our shield and leave us frightfully exposed.

I am keenly aware of those feelings in myself. When I've been hurt in any way, I'm leery of that person for a while. Remember the old adage, "Hurt me once, shame on you. Hurt me twice, shame on me." Why would I ever put myself in a position to trust again so you can hurt me a second time . . . or third, or thirtieth, or two hundredth?

Well, we *would* be idiots to put ourselves in vulnerable positions time after time. For example, if I find that my friend Violet steals things, I'm not going to leave her alone with my jewelry box. That would be dumb. I can still like her, though.

If I've confided in Claudia and later find out that she divulged my secret to her book club, I've just learned not to confide in Claudia again. But I can forgive her and continue enjoying her as a friend. I don't have to hold a grudge or reject her, or tell everyone else how rotten Claudia is. I can just quietly decide to forgive. Even better, I can tell her my feelings. She might benefit from that information, and she would know me better.

"Claudia, when I found out you told the book club

what I'd told you in confidence, I was really upset and angry with you. I thought you'd keep your promise not to tell. But I've had some time to adjust to it, and I forgive you. It won't stop our friendship, that's for sure."

Then, hopefully, I would let it go. Keeping that hurt alive benefits no one at all, certainly not me. The next time we met I could genuinely hug her with affection and go on with our relationship as if nothing had jarred it.

Admittedly, that's the ideal. Often I've not been able to forgive someone nearly that easily or quickly. In fact, more often than not it's been extremely difficult. But I see progress, and that's what's important. I see clearly how I *want* to act and feel. I get a little closer to that attitude each time I have to draw on my forgiving expertise.

Mostly I'm encouraged at finding that forgiving benefits *me*.

Let's assume you already knew that. You agree that holding grudges is a waste of time. You, too, want to let go and get back to loving. You're able to forgive friends and family with ease.

And then one day you discover your wife or husband has had an affair.

What do you do?

Naturally that's a heavy blow; one of the heaviest life deals out. Almost everyone feels enormous hurt, followed quickly by tremendous rage. So many feelings come into play. There is betrayal, shock, rejection, fear, indeed practically every negative feeling we're capable of experiencing.

The procedure at that point depends on your mate's intentions. Some wives or husbands having affairs are already on the way out of the marriage and have no intention or desire to get the marriage back into shape. They want a divorce. There might be little or no remorse because their hearts are already "married" to the new lover.

We'll deal with that in a later chapter. But many times the errant wife (or husband, but for now let's say it's the wife) is almost relieved to have been caught. She's embarrassed, ashamed and sorry the whole thing happened. She explains how she got caught up in it, she apologizes, and she says, "Will you forgive me? I promise you it's over and I learned something from it; I love you more than I could love anyone else. I want it all behind us. It'll never happen again."

Now what do you do?

Maybe you believe her. You know her so well that you can read what's going on in her head. You know she's sorry, you know it's over and she loves you, not the other guy. You're glad she's back on the right track.

But it would be a rare person, indeed, who could say, "Sure, sweetie, I forgive you immediately and completely. From now on it's behind us. Let's just forget it. I love you, too."

That's asking an awful lot.

Wounded mates are usually so devastated at that point they wonder if they *ever* can forgive, and they *know* they can't forget.

Their emotions are shot. They feel and act like accident victims in intensive care. Their spirits are bruised and beaten, and they ache all over.

They alternate between feelings of love and relief, and feelings of anger and fear. They bounce back and forth. One moment they want to cry with joy and make passionate love. The next, they want to strike back and punish like they've been hurt.

They can think of nothing else. Their days and nights are filled with imagining scenes between the lovers. They hunger for details of it, and they feel sickened at thinking about it. There is almost no peace of mind. They're haunted by the fear that maybe the other person was a better lover and now nothing will ever be good enough. They're defeated, inflamed and enraged.

Forgive? They wouldn't know how to begin, even if they wanted to. The hurt is too intense.

The mate who cheated is usually very repentant at first, wanting only to be forgiven and have the marriage "back to normal." It's the mate who was cheated on who is not willing to drop the issue yet . . . sometimes not for a long, long time. It seems to be the only topic of conversation in that household. Nothing else is important anymore.

A typical conversation between a husband and wife who's found out about his affair might go like this:

She: More coffee?

He: No thanks. It was a great dinner, honey.

She: As good as *HER* dinners were?

He: Oh, please, do we have to talk about that again?

She: What do you expect? I find out you're in love with another woman and I'm supposed to act like it never happened? It *did* happen, damn it. How do I know it isn't still going on?

He: Because I've told you it's over, and I mean it. I don't know what else I can say. It's over, that's all. How long do we have to keep hashing it over?

She: As long as it takes, that's how long. Until I can believe in you again. I trusted you and you broke that trust. I can't just pretend it never happened. All day long when you're at work I wonder if you're calling her or if she's calling you. I can't work anymore. All day long I think about you and her. And you expect me not to talk about it? I can't believe you!

He: Honey, it's over. It's a dead issue. I learned something. I'm not about to let it happen again . . . ever. All I can do is promise you I won't call her . . . I won't talk to her even if she calls me.

She: She is calling you, then?

He: No! She isn't . . . she won't. She knows it's over.

She: How does she know? Have you been talking to her?

He: (sighing) No . . . not since the day you found out. I called her and told her it was over and I wouldn't see or talk to her anymore . . . and she shouldn't try to contact me, either. I told you that.

She: And you expect me to believe you after what you've done?

He: Look, I feel totally helpless. I tell you the truth and you don't believe me, anyway. Why do we keep talking about it? It doesn't get us anywhere.

She: Because I'm so profoundly hurt, that's why. You don't seem to realize what you've done to me . . . to us. I'm not sure I can ever forget it.

And so on. The conversation goes on and on in the same vein, getting no place, leaving both parties frustrated and discouraged.

But it's easy to understand both sides. She *can't* trust him. He *can't* seem to reassure her. They're stuck in a miserable place.

I generally suggest that they do need to talk about it, but it might be helpful to limit the conversations on this subject to so many minutes a day. I might say, "It would be almost impossible for Karen *not* to talk about the affair. She's too scared and too hurt. But you're right, Mike, that going over and over it isn't doing either of you any good, either. How about you both determining how much time every day you want to discuss it and limiting this topic to only that much time, say, 20 minutes a day at first. Every day for 20 minutes Karen can talk about it, ask you questions, tell you off, describe her fears and her feelings, ask for reassurance, for 20 minutes straight.

"Then, when the time is up, the subject is closed for the day. You're free to talk about other things, go someplace, do something fun. It would be great if you put some fun back into your lives. You've suffered enough, you two. How about taking dancing lessons, going to basketball games or having a dinner party?"

Mike is tickled to death with my suggestion, because 20 minutes a day sounds like heaven compared to the relentless pursuing of the subject up to now. Karen is generally reluctant to agree to this. "I can't just shut it off the rest of the day," she says.

"You can *think* about it if you want," I tell her. "You might even want to write in a journal. Put down all your feelings; write out your anger and define your fears. It'll be an interesting book to share with someone going through the same thing someday, if you ever feel like it. It might help them so that they'll get over it eventually."

Karen agrees, with some misgivings, and we make another appointment. Usually they report that it helped, when they return the next week. Often Mike is saying, "I think we could cut down to 10 minutes a day," and Karen rejects that idea. For her it's been extremely hard to stop at 20 minutes, and understandably so. She sees this as a dangerous and insidious disease that's attacked their marriage. She's frightened out of her wits that history will repeat itself; that she'll never again be able to relax and trust like she did before.

She doesn't *want* to let it go at this point. She wants just the opposite; to make life so miserable for him that he'll never, ever let himself even consider cheating again.

In addition to the very normal fears she's experiencing, she probably wants a little revenge on him for messing up her life so horribly. She still has a need to punish him.

Is she wrong? Probably not. But is it doing her any good? Also, probably not. Certainly she has a right to her hurt and anger, and she also has the right and the responsibility to tell him her feelings.

But at some point it becomes non-productive. There's no new information being traded, no new insights to help with understanding and empathy. It's all been said. To continue discussing it only belabors the issue and flogs the dead horse.

The long-punished guilty person begins getting resentful of the relentless punishing from the innocent one. "He deserves every bit of discomfort he feels," many people would say. Hell hath no fury as a woman scorned—or a man, either.

Sometimes I ask, "How long do you want to stay angry with this person?"

The answer is usually a puzzled, "Well, how do *I* know?"

"Well," I suggest, "what would be the length of time you'd recommend to your best friend? How long should someone else stay angry for this same kind of offense? A month? A year? Three years? Forever?"

Frequently, the person thinks about it and says, "I don't *want* to stay angry at all, I really don't. I just can't seem to let it go. I'm scared to relax, I think. I'm afraid to trust again. I can't help it."

I understand those fears. The important thing is that now there is at least a tiny desire to get back to normal. "I don't want to stay angry at all" is a healthy step. Once we have the *desire* to let anger go we can begin to do it, even if we take tiny baby steps.

I have total faith in anyone's ability to achieve forgiveness once they decide that's what they want to do. The decision is a giant step in itself.

Perhaps the word "forgive" means something like "I don't want to stay angry at all" or "I'd like to be able to let it go." Forgiving doesn't mean condoning bad behavior. Often we're reluctant to forgive for fear it will imply we think the behavior was okay after all. But that's not what it means, not at all.

What does it mean, then?

One possibility is the saying, "Hate the sin but love the sinner." I can disapprove strongly of something you might have done, but I can love you just as dearly as if you'd never done it at all.

To me that's been easiest to do with our children. Parental love is so strong that most of us are easily able to forgive our children for practically anything, especially if they admit to making a mistake and are sorry about it. It's harder with adults who are not our flesh and blood.

So, perhaps it's the *love* that enables us to forgive, more than the circumstances or logic involved. If I love you, I'm going to want to forgive you much sooner than if I didn't love you.

"I did love her," said one cheated-on husband, "but she killed that love when she slept with that other guy. I can't love her anymore."

That's not an unusual feeling, but it needn't continue if the man *wants* to love again. You've probably seen the posters that say, "Love is not a feeling but a decision." Sometimes we need to decide, consciously, that we want to love, in order to open ourselves up for the feelings we once knew as "love." To act in a loving way, even if we don't feel like it, can actually increase our love for a mate, and the mate is quite likely to respond.

What if a mate is not very loveable? If we wait for him to act loveably it might take a long, long time, but we don't have to wait. We can start loving even if the other person isn't ready. We get to love anytime, and we can love anyone. That's a privilege no one can take from us.

I need only to decide I want to love you, and then begin to act as if I already do. Have you noticed how many movie actors fall in love with their costars? Over the years there have been quite a few. I suspect the "acting in love" makes the process happen in fact.

We get to "play movie star!" I know I'm oversimplifying, but I truly believe we can set upon any course of action we choose, and our feelings will follow. Feelings follow action.

Give your energy to anger and punishment and your feelings will stay stuck there. Focus the energy on loving or acting as if you're loving, and you'll fall in love before long at all.

The choice is ours. And our enjoyment of life will be determined largely by the choice we make. If I choose to stay angry, keep the hurt alive, punish, reject and process the injustice someone has done over and over and over, I'm going to keep myself miserable.

If I choose to *want* to forgive, let go of the whole thing, act as if I love and keep my energy active on "loving the sinner," I'm going to be a whole lot happier.

It hasn't got much to do with the other person. *I* am the one choosing my behavior. The way *I* act and think will determine my state of mind. I would hope always to opt for the forgiving stance, rather than harboring resentment.

What if I forgive and love again, and then he has another affair and hurts me again? A valid question and one worth considering. We have to decide for ourselves how many of those we're willing to tolerate. Some will say, "One. After that the marriage is over."

I'm not sure how I feel because I've never had to face that problem in my own marriage. I know legally I'd have no problem divorcing an unfaithful husband. Even morally it would be understood by my church. Society would understand and probably condone divorce under that circumstance, in almost any culture or religion.

But it's nice to know *I* get to make that decision regardless of anyone else's principles or rules. I might choose to forgive a couple of times, I don't know. I think it would depend on how repentant my husband would be, and how much I value the marriage.

I know some men who would die before they would ever be unfaithful, but in other ways they're jerks. Staying faithful doth not necessarily a good husband (or wife) make. Anyone can make a mistake, even two or three mistakes, and still be a gem.

I think sometimes we make too much of infidelity, setting it up as "the unforgiveable sin," when maybe it needn't be. Interestingly, my experience has been that a woman will forgive a husband's cheating far more often than a man will forgive a wife's. I don't know why.

Women feel just as devastated and shattered as men do at the discovery of an affair, but in my observations, they've been more willing to let the pain go and try harder to work on the marriage. Men have usually seemed so angered they're ready to junk the marriage on the spot.

But one can't generalize, I know. Every person decides what he or she would do if their spouse had an affair. I can't tell you what's right for you.

I know what I would want to do, and that's to forgive this wrong just as I've forgiven all the others.

But please understand that I'm not condoning infidelity. Nor do I condone lying, stealing or even cheating on history tests. However, I've done all three. Although I've regretted doing them, I learned something important: They caused me more unhappiness than happiness.

Most of us have done *many* things that go against our moral belief system. Yet, at the time, we seemed to find justification for them. Often it's been after the fact that we find the reasons we shouldn't have done them.

Sometimes we know full well we shouldn't be doing whatever it is we're going to do, yet we do it anyway. I smile at the statement Lisa made one say when she was excitedly planning a trip to an expensive resort in Sedona that she couldn't afford. "There is no justification to my spending that kind of money," she admitted, "so I won't even try to justify it. I'll just do it."

We all do things we can't justify. If we learn from them they're probably good for us, unless they've hurt someone else in the process. When we do hurt someone, either accidentally or deliberately, we need to apologize and make restitution to that person if possible.

Then we need to forgive ourselves.

That's difficult, too. Sometimes we hang onto guilt long after it's necessary. A little healthy guilt is good for us, and I disagree with those who say it's needless. If I hurt you I *should* feel guilty!

But what I do with guilt is the important thing. If I use it to remind me that other people are not to be trifled with, not to be disrespected without discomfort on both sides, it's a healthy reminder. If I use it as impetus to try to make restitution, it's positive. If I use it as fuel to keep myself miserable, it's unhealthy. And sometimes we do just that. We go over and over in our minds some incident that we regret, keeping ourselves in a continuous snit of regret and remorse, kicking ourselves when we're down, punishing ourselves relentlessly . . . to absolutely no avail.

It's useless behavior. What's done is done. Sometimes

we fall victim to a state called *scrupulosity,* in which we are excessive in our self-punishment.

I once had a client who married quite young, and she and her husband had used recreational drugs pretty foolishly. In one of her mind-altered states she'd slept with a friend of his, and at the time it seemed the okay thing to do. But as she got older and smarter she looked back at that incident with a lot of regret.

It became an obsession with her. She stewed about it constantly, even dreaming about it at night. She confessed it to her rabbi, her father, her mother and finally her husband. She saw one or two counselors before she came to me. All of us told her virtually the same thing. "It's over. It was wrong, but you saw that and quit the drugs that led you into it. It can be forgotten, now."

Easy for us to say. She couldn't forget it. She believed that God loved her, understood and forgave her, but she still wouldn't forgive herself.

When we flat can't (or won't) forgive ourselves we need to look for the "payoff" we're getting for keeping that unnecessary guilt alive. That kind of guilt is neurotic guilt; a useless, crippling state that does us way more harm than good.

Usually, the reason we hold onto guilt is for the false sense of "goodness" it gives us. Our unconscious rationale is something like this: "I must be a very, very, very good person to feel this guilty this long. My pain and suffering prove how noble and worthy I am. This intense discomfort makes me morally superior to those who might do wrong and promptly forgive themselves. I refuse to forgive myself in order to elevate myself above the rest."

Now, of course, that's not thought out at a conscious level. In fact, people who get into that state of unrelenting guilt see themselves as distinctly unworthy. But frequently, if they can see that they're holding onto the guilt to make themselves feel "very, very, very good," they might become willing to let it go and join the rest of us ordinary people who do dumb things and feel guilty, but finally forgive ourselves.

We need to forgive—ourselves and others. Remember the line in the Lord's Prayer that says, "Forgive us our trespasses as we forgive others?" What if it said, "Forgive us our trespasses as much as (and no more than) we forgive others?" Or "as much and no more than we forgive ourselves." I wonder if that would be more of an incentive to forgive.

Again, religion and mental health go hand in hand, as they so often do. Whether we look at forgiveness as something taught by our spiritual leaders, or as an attitude that's going to make us *feel* better, we're going to be happier people when we forgive than when we don't.

C h a p t e r   1 1

And Baby Makes Three

First of all I will establish this very crucial fact: Having four children and helping them grow up to be happy, healthy adults is the most meaningful achievement in my whole life. Nothing else means as much.

The entire wall space on both sides of our hallway is filled with pictures: Laurie and Lisa on one wall, Lindsay and Lyle on the other. I like to stand in the hall brushing my teeth and gaze at them in maternal adoration. I treasure each child and offer God a fervent thank-you for them at least once a day.

But . . . it was a big job.

As every parent knows, the time and energy needed to rear a child boggles the mind. Are they worth it? They are to me. Should everyone have children? I sure don't think so, any more than I think everyone should get married.

But when we are parents, it's really helpful to learn some things that will make the job easier. Most of us graduate from school, find work, marry our prince or princess and have our first babies without ever having a class on parenting. It would never occur to us that we need one. We assume parenting comes naturally, if we ever think about it at all.

When we do think about it, it's usually in lovely fanta-sies. On starry nights with the boy or girl of our dreams we revel in imagining the wonder of how it would be. "If we get married would you want children?"

"Of course . . . a little girl just like you."

"And I want a boy like you. Oh, won't they be cute? Maybe we should have four or five. I love kids, don't you?"

"Sure, they're neat."

On one of those starry nights Larry and I took it a step further by suggesting, "Wouldn't it be fun if we all had names that start with 'L'?" I wiggled with the joy of it all. And so we did what we set out to do. Every year we take pictures for Christmas cards, with the entire family look-ing rested, happy and as though there's nothing we'd rather be doing than posing together. People may even think we always look that way.

I hereby publicly admit we don't. (But by now the Christmas card picture is a tradition that can't be dropped because all the cards are framed in the hall next to the girls' and boys' pictures.)

But what did Larry and I know when we brought the first baby home from the hospital? Zilch. Nada. We didn't know a whole lot more when we brought home the sec-ond, third, or even the fourth.

Now we're experts, as are most grandparents. By the time we no longer need the skills, we've got them down pat. How did we learn? By making jillions of mistakes.

Fortunately there are lots of books on parenting these days. Almost every women's magazine has an article on parenting. (I wonder why they seem to be lacking in men's magazines.)

Some churches and schools offer parenting classes. Such classes are particularly helpful because parents get to hear other parents talk about their problems and find out they're not alone. All parents struggle to do the best they can.

But a book on marriage wouldn't be complete without a chapter on the joys and trials of parenthood. After all, now that I'm an expert I want to use my skills a *little* bit!

It starts out pretty easily. The days of feeling queasy and tired are all part of the excitement to a first-time mother. It's such fun telling everybody, "We're going to have a baby!" that both the woman and the man feel a nice importance, like they've done something pretty special. Indeed they have. There's nothing more special than a human life.

Sharing the experience of the birth is one of the most profound occasions a couple will ever have. Usually they feel very close during those first few days in the hospital.

When they take the baby home they're thrilled beyond words. And the excitement is compounded by friends and family coming by with gifts and good wishes, and everyone agreeing that the baby is the marvel of the century.

The next few months, however, are some of the toughest they'll ever face. Unless the baby is highly unusual, he or she cries a goodly amount and seems to need hours and hours of care. According to a pediatrician I know, the care requires seven hours a day. How do you find seven extra hours every day?

You give up any free time you might have had before. Pretty soon you begin to get tired and cranky. You feel like you haven't had a full night's sleep in years, though it's been only weeks. There's a sinking fear that life may never be the same again. Both parents feel haggard; both believe they need and deserve a little time for themselves.

They get testy with each other. At times they're even resentful of the baby, which causes them to feel guilty and think they must be awful people.

For the most part sex goes out the window for a while, partly due to the woman's physical condition, but even more because of her emotional indifference to sex. It's not permanent, but the husband begins to think it is. The more frustrated he becomes the more resentful he is.

The new mother is enchanted with the sensual feelings she experiences at feeling the baby's skin against hers. She had no idea it would be so heady a relationship. The innate love she feels toward the newborn child finds her totally unprepared. She knew she'd love her baby, but she hadn't an inkling of how much.

Neither did her husband. He feels more than a bit miffed at her endless cuddling, and sometimes grows weary of the baby being their only topic of conversation these days. While sex might have been equally important to both before, it's a rare wife who continues feeling erotic at the same level *after* she gives birth.

Again, I emphasize that this turned-off state is temporary. The danger comes only if one or both parties fear it will be this way from now on, because fear escalates the problem.

As the husband watches his wife's love affair with the baby he feels distinctly unimportant to her. He may or may not express his threatened feelings, but those very natural feelings of rejection will probably surface in some way. She'll feel the disapproval in his manner and become uncomfortable about it. She knows exactly what's causing it, but she feels helpless to try to change. So intense is her feeling of responsibility for this new person in her life that it seems unthinkable to focus less attention on the baby.

Nevertheless, she knows she has a certain responsibility toward her husband, too, and so sometimes sex becomes "a duty." She wants to be a good wife. She does love her husband. So she may initiate sex some nights even though she's exhausted and longing for sleep. Perhaps it's not terribly rewarding to either of them. That causes them to worry about it even more.

If I could give young parents my best advice it would be this: As much as you can, convince yourselves that this is only a temporary setback in the sexual arena. The only thing you have to fear is fear itself, because that fear becomes the real deterrent by mushrooming into a Giant Problem.

It doesn't have to.

When you know what to expect, you handle it much more easily than when you don't. For instance, knowing that children will lose their baby teeth makes that process one we take in stride. If we *didn't* know it was normal, we might feel tremendous concern. "How will my child be able to chew?"

It's that same unnecessary fright that young parents endure over the question of sex. "Will we never again feel the passion and desire we've always had before?"

If you know it's a passing phase that everyone else has survived, you can see it as a minor irritant, but nothing to get in a snit over. Libido returns, as do teeth. Trust the process.

However, if the sexual relationship does *not* return after a few months, you'll know there's some other problem to deal with. One or both partners may be choking off a normal desire for sex because of reasons that have little or nothing to do with the new baby. The problem may be pent-up, unresolved anger. It's virtually impossible to experience anger and sexual desire at the same time, so we have to resolve the hostility before the desire can return.

In fact, it's easy to blame the birth of a baby for the deterioration of a relationship, but it's not usually the baby's fault. If the relationship suffers any major setbacks they're more likely caused by a lack of communication. When we keep sharing respectfully with each other, *all* feelings should proceed in a nice healthy way, including sexual ones.

Still, the warm, romantic interludes are generally quite diminished for a few weeks or months. That fact along with the seemingly constant demands of the infant can put a real strain on the relationship.

I suppose it would be lessened if one could afford a Mary Poppins-like nanny who would tend to the needs of the wee one, freeing the parents to go off by themselves and have fun without worrying about the kid. But most of us can't afford that lifestyle.

We should try to get breaks when we can, though. Asking a neighbor or friend to baby-sit is good sense. Children are happier when their parents love each other, so we do them a big favor by having fun ourselves. We're definitely *not* uncaring parents when we get a trusted sitter and go out for a few hours. On the contrary, we're adding to our store of mental health, which will benefit rather than harm the baby.

But even without a child to complicate our lives, there is usually a gradual lessening of the intensity of sex. Indeed, marriage itself often marks a certain reduction in sexuality between two people who used to be extremely sexual together. You may have heard that the best method of birth control is "marriage," because you quit having sex. Hopefully it's a joke, but there's a certain amount of truth in it. Forbidden fruit is always the most appealing, and once it's there for us in abundance, it often loses some of its attractiveness.

A couple who are truly committed to each other and the principle of marriage needn't worry that their love lives are down the drain just because there are children added.

Communication with lots of honesty and respect should clear the way for genuine warmth and love, including plenty of romantic love. Both people need to feel perfectly free to express all their feelings, even the "bad" ones. Remember, feelings are never right or wrong.

It's perfectly appropriate to say, "I find myself feeling resentful of how much time the baby takes."

Or, "I miss the days when it was just you and me alone together."

Or, "I feel like second fiddle. All your love seems to be directed at the baby."

Or, "I'm hurt that you don't seem to love the baby as much as I thought you would."

Or, "I don't want always to have to be the one who feeds her in the night."

Or, "It feels like our romantic days are over, and I'm scared to death."

Or, "You seem disinterested in me and the baby."

Or, "It makes me mad that you refuse to change a diaper."

Expressing our feelings helps us feel better, but there's no guarantee that we'll get new behavior right away. Still, having expressed ourselves, we know we've planted a seed of information that might sprout into a positive change later on.

And even if we never get results, we're happier in letting our feelings be known than in hiding them and pretending everything's fine. *That* is the sure-fire killer of sexual desire!

To feel understood is such a precious gift, and one we

can give each other even when we can't immediately solve a problem. Our tendency is often to jump in and defend ourselves or argue about the other person's feelings. We want to say, "You shouldn't feel that way!"

Reminding ourselves that feelings are *not* right or wrong might help us accept them in ourselves as well as in the other person. The immediate need is not so much to find a solution as it is to share some feelings and understand each other.

Let's use this statement as an example: "I miss the days when it was just you and me alone together."

Some possible responses:

"You jerk! You think you should be the center of the universe all the time, don't you? Well, you're going to have to share me for a long time, so you'd better get used to it."

Or, "Yeah, well, everybody has to grow up sometime."

Or, "You shouldn't feel that way! You should love the baby and be glad we have him!"

Or, "You sound like a selfish little kid."

Or, "Then why did you agree that we should have a family in the first place?"

Or, "You think *I* like it?"

The understanding response would allow the feelings, accept them and also express your own:

"I know. It *was* nice when it was just the two of us, wasn't it? But this is nice in a different way, to me. The baby will need less time, little by little. I hope you know I still love you!"

Why is it so hard to respond that way? We love each other. We love the baby. We want to be kind. And yet, so often, we lash out in an attacking kind of response.

An attack of any kind comes from someone who feels afraid or victimized. It's easy to empathize with the fear both parents feel. Usually, the new mother is so captivated by her new role that she's threatened at the thought of having to "give up her love affair." Any criticism from her husband sets up alarms in her head that she might be asked to change her focus back on him.

From his viewpoint, of course, there's fear that he's lost his friend, lover and playmate. She's so different now. So from that vantage point of fright, both partners act out in anger, pouting, withdrawal or distancing.

It helps so much to know that unloving behavior is almost invariably coming from the position of fear. It makes it so much more tolerable and non-threatening. I can understand and love you, and feel compassion for you when I know your bad behavior stems from fear. Hopefully you can react the same in the face of my bad behavior. To reassure the fear often takes care of the disrespect.

But all of us can spout wise sayings and preach mentally healthy responses when we're calm, comfortable, relaxed, rested and unpressured. We're *never* in that state when we have a new baby around the house! So, we're vulnerable to overreacting, getting our feelings hurt, feeling victimized and wanting revenge. It goes with the territory. We wouldn't want it that way, but it happens. Again, it's like the flu. We get it and we get over it, and we're happier when we're able not to give it too much importance in our lives.

The tiredness and apprehension that come with the baby go away. We get to keep the good part; that marvel of the century!

Chapter 12

What's a Parent To Do?

P arenting wasn't nearly as confusing in the "olden days." Parents didn't worry much about children's feelings. Rules such as "Children should be seen and not heard" were widely held, and physical punishment was the norm. Kids knew where they stood. Father was the head of the house, and the words "Wait till your father gets home" struck terror into little misbehaving hearts.

There were kind fathers, of course, as well as kind mothers, but one thing was believed by parents and children alike: parents were the bosses and children were submissive. If you knew what was good for you you didn't make waves.

And it worked. By and large kids minded parents. Today it's a whole different world. Why? Back in the days of yore when there were powerful people running the world, kings lorded it over the "lesser folk." They made rules like, "If you disobey our laws you get your head chopped off," and the poor peons knew they meant business. After seeing a few of their friends lose their heads, the ordinary folk wisely minded the rules.

But there were always a few brave souls willing to risk

their lives, and now and then they would revolt. There was always a revolution someplace, and many of them were fights for equality. It took hundreds of years for human rights to become a rather common issue, and for most of those years men stayed "superior" to women. Everybody knew their place.

Father was the chief boss, followed by subservient mother, and kids were the peons with no rights at all. The system worked up until World War II, when women had to (or got to) go out in droves to work in war plants and such. Rosie the Riveter changed things for good.

Women came back to tend the home fires when the war was over, but they no longer believed that their husbands were more important than they. They felt "just as good" after their exposure to the outside world. And most of them got downright cocky and dared to challenge men's supremacy.

Whether or not men believed women were equal to them didn't matter; the women believed it and acted accordingly. No longer willing to "mind" their husbands blindly, they began to do things to prove their own importance.

My own father looked askance at wives' working outside the home. When my mother decided she was going to work anyway he was not pleased. But they needed the money; their teenage children were self-reliant; and, of course, Mama agreed that she'd still cook a grand dinner every night and the housework wouldn't suffer. Off she went to an office for eight hours a day. Dad could see that things were no longer the same, and he reluctantly accepted the changes.

My mom was one of many thousands. She was influenced by other wives who were declaring their independence, and they encouraged one another. They got to enjoy the heady feeling of earning money, which gave them some power in decision making that they'd never before enjoyed. Some men still resented it, but they began to see they were fighting a losing battle. No longer would women feel or act like they were of lesser importance.

That was the revolution that ended men's superiority, but there was still a major revolution to come—the children's. Little boys and girls all over the country watched as Mom became "as good as" Dad. They watched equality raise its head, and they couldn't help but like the idea!

They began their own revolt with the belief, "If Mom is as good as Dad, then I'm just as good as them both!"

Whether or not Mom and Dad agreed was unimportant, the fact was already established in the children's minds. No longer were they willing to be submissive and subservient. Just as men had struggled against women's rebellion, parents now struggled against their children's emerging strength, but it was too great a force to be held off.

Society was now completely withdrawing from the old-fashioned autocratic system. Some of us might wish it were still in existence, but it's gone and we can't wish it back.

What does that mean, then? Surely as parents we still have the right to make the rules and see that our laws are carried out! We'll "chop off their heads" if they disobey! We'll punish them, by God.

And we may, but in our children's minds is the strong belief, "If you have the right to punish us, we have the right to punish you," and you may already know how good they are at this.

The harder we punish them the more ways they can find to get back at us. Though punishment can often be effective with very young children, it loses all effectiveness as they grow older. In fact, it will have served only to demonstrate that *power* gives us permission to "lord it over" others. The most autocratic, powerful, punishing parents are surely rearing the most rebellious, powerful, punishing children.

If we're smart, then, we have to find other ways to teach our children. Certainly we can't relinquish our responsibility and let them do as they please. But gone are the days when reward and punishment were the best teachers.

Fortunately there are wonderful skills that can be easily learned, and they're so much more effective than the old punishing ways. Today's children who are lucky enough to get the benefit of the newer methods of discipline will almost certainly grow up to be more responsible than if they'd been "punished into submission."

They'll also grow up mentally healthy. In the olden days, mental health was not necessarily the norm. People did conform, yes, but inwardly they did a lot of unhealthy resenting and rebelling in insidious ways. They weren't honest and respectful with each other. They lived illusions of being happy families, but there was a great amount of unhappiness in their lives, too.

Disrespect was the order of business in the olden days. The process of life was finding one's place in the hierarchy and living accordingly, even if it violated human rights.

It's marvelous that we've come so far in our awareness that people shouldn't be mistreated. Society needed that realization. But when parents bought the concept of respecting children, they sometimes went overboard in the other direction.

They swung from being tough, controlling, punishing, autocratic parents to being wimpy, overprotective and permissive, which was no doubt worse.

The one good thing about autocratic systems is that at least there is some sense of order, with everyone knowing his limits.

There is probably *nothing* good about the permissive system. All it does is teach children that the world is there to serve them. Children of permissive parents don't learn self-discipline or responsibility. They become greedy and selfish and unable to deal with the real world. They are dependent on others and resentful of those on whom they depend. All in all they're the most abused of any children, because they're deprived of learning their own sense of self-reliance and the value of work and discipline. Work is worth. We need to have work in order to feel good about ourselves, whether we're astronauts or three-year-olds dusting the piano.

Permissive parents have the best of intentions, raising children with "love." But unless their love includes discipline and responsibility, it's not very loving. When children are given whatever they want, they come to believe that's how life should be, which is a sadly distorted view of the universe. In permissive homes children are the tyrants who rule, and parents are the lowly peons, there only to serve.

All right, so what do we do? We don't want the old autocratic ways anymore, which taught disrespect by punishing and produced rebellious young adults who determined to control and humiliate as they'd been controlled and humiliated. Nor do we want permissive homes that produce weak, demanding tyrants who collapse when faced with the challenges of real life.

We want, instead, strong children who grow up to be responsible and healthy, physically, mentally and emotionally. We want them to be able to make good decisions in all the facets of their life: work, family and society.

We want them to pull their own weight, not being merely "takers" who lean on others. We want them to learn assertiveness and develop the confidence to go after what they want, respecting their own needs as well as everyone else's.

In order to become that kind of adult, they have to learn early in their lives how to make decisions. The only way to develop good decision-making expertise is to *make decisions,* whether good or bad.

So the kind of home we want for our children's best possible development is a democratic one, in which there is honesty and respect, and plenty of opportunity to make decisions. We want our children to decide all kinds of things for themselves, learning values as they go.

As a rule of thumb, I like the 2-9-18 formula, in which you let a two-year-old make two decisions out of every 18, a nine-year-old make nine decisions out of every 18, and so on.

Assume that in a typical morning there are roughly 18 choices that affect your two-year-old's life. He gets to make two of them, and you make the rest. At age two he's capable of deciding whether he wants to wear his green sweater or his red sweater out to play. You decide whether or not he needs a sweater at all, but he gets to choose which one. You decide to serve juice for breakfast, but he may choose between apple and orange juice. You decide when he takes his nap, but he may choose which animal he takes to bed with him.

By making those decisions at an early age he's already on the road to making bigger decisions. So at nine-years old he's capable of making nine out of 18, or half of his decisions.

By then he's such a pro at choosing options we can enjoy the pride we feel at watching his good judgement.

How did he get so good? By making 9000 dumb decisions in his early years, and having to live with the consequences. When he makes a choice and he's not happy with the result, he's just learned something useful—not to make that same choice next time.

A child who gets to make so many of his own decisions gets very skilled at it, so that by age 18 he's perfectly capable of making 18 out of 18 decisions. In other words, all of them.

If we've done our job well we can watch our 18-year-olds graduate from high school and feel strongly confident in their ability to go out in the world and live productive lives. That's really what all of us want for our children.

But out of our mistaken beliefs, we often cripple them with overprotection. We rescue them from their bad choices, we remind and nag, and we virtually live their lives for them, so that at age 18 they're no more equipped to handle life than they were at age two.

And then we shake our heads with worry and say, "This kid has no sense at all. She's simply not a responsible person. And after all we've done for her!"

Those of you with children under two have a great advantage. But even if your children are older, it's never too late to initiate this process. They'll still be way ahead of children who never get the benefit of learning responsible decision making.

A word of warning, however: It's hard to do. Because we love these children so much, we hate to see them hurting in any way. Our empathy for them is so fine-tuned and our compassion for their discomfort so strong that it takes all the restraint we've got to keep from rescuing them. We know so well what's good for them, and we want to protect them from any pain they might encounter by making mistakes.

So we teach them exactly what they should do in every situation. Then we remind them over and over. In case they didn't hear us the first time, we make sure to remind them a third time, a 29th and a 63rd.

We take responsibility for their lives, doing them a dreadful disservice. How much more loving we are when we respect them enough to let them make choices, knowing they're smart and that they'll learn from good and bad choices alike.

My friend and mentor Dr. Oscar Christensen uses the example of an ordinary breakfast as a setting for teaching. I offer his illustration:

"I would not give a two-year-old the decision as to whether to play with my shotgun or not. But I might be so bold as to allow a choice of cereal in the morning, whether it be Crispy Critters or Cheerios—he decides.

"As you probably guessed, the traditional mother would have given the youngster oatmeal in the first place because she knows that is best. After three bites of oatmeal, the child refuses to finish. Then begins the process of reward and punishment, the traditional approach for making the child eat. Mother begins with bribery.

"'Honey bunch, this is yummy stuff; now eat this gruel; it is good for you.' 'You'll love it. Eat this and you can have some toast with sugar on it.' 'Eat this and I'll give you a dime.' 'Eat this or I'll hit you.' That is the full routine for an autocratic approach. Finally, the last punishment: 'Okay, bad kid, down from the table.'

"Now, on the other extreme, the permissive mother would give the child two bites of oatmeal, two bites of cereal, two bites of egg, two bites of anything else he wants and finally at 11:30 she would get disgusted and send him from the table and wonder why he didn't eat lunch.

"The mother we are trying to create is the one who says, 'You decide, Crispy Critters or Cheerios?' But once the milk is poured, the decision is irreversible. You can't re-crisp a soggy critter. This is his breakfast and this is the decision the child has to live with. If any of you have dallied over your prepared cereals in the morning, you will recall that within a very short period of time they can become worse than the oatmeal in appearance and texture. Therefore, I would make a fairly safe prediction that ultimately this youngster too would come to the same conclusion that his breakfast is not edible.

"At this time, mother would give him his second choice of the morning, 'Either eat the cereal or excuse yourself; you decide.' Now chances are the youngster will jump down from the table in glee because he didn't have to eat the cereal. At that point, mother may say, 'I see you have decided to excuse yourself.'

"Those of you with any experience at all know that at 10:00 both of the youngsters are going to be back; they are both going to be hungry; they are both going to be nasty to live with. The oatmeal non-eater comes back to mother and says, 'Okay, you dumb old mother you, I am hungry and it's your fault. It's your fault. You sent me from the table.' Unfortunately, there's just enough truth in the statement that mother typically feels guilty and gives him 40 graham crackers before sending him out to play.

"The mother I'm trying to create is the one who, when the child comes back at 10:00 to complain of his hunger, says, 'Yes, I'll bet you are. It's probably because you didn't finish your breakfast this morning. Maybe tomorrow you will. Now run along and play; I'll see you at lunch.'

"Regardless of how mother handled the situation, it is my contention that both children learned. There is no

such thing as a non-learning child. Both children learned.
The oatmeal non-eater learned he can do anything he
wants to do so long as he demonstrates that it is someone
else's fault."

One of our biggest temptations is to rescue our children from the consequences of their choices. Sometimes I
think if we all switched kids and raised each other's we
wouldn't get so tuned in on rescuing, because we have a
better sense of perspective with other children. Our own
are too precious to us. We too often refuse to allow them
to experience any discomfort at all, even if it's healthy for
them.

I confess to having been one of the most overprotective mothers. When counselors pointed out the harm I
was inflicting on our children I was disbelieving at first,
but I finally came to see they were right. That was the first
time I realized we can't always trust "common sense."

If you're not sure just when you "overprotect" or "rescue," an example of my own overprotective days may
help. In second grade Laurie played often with our little
neighbor, Debbie. One September afternoon they were
playing in our back yard, when suddenly I heard raised
voices, then tears. Laurie raced into the kitchen wailing
that she and Debbie had found an autumn leaf in our back
yard and had reached for it at the same time. Debbie maintained she'd seen it first, so it should be hers; Laurie
claimed ownership on the grounds it was in her yard.
They'd fought over it, and Debbie had taken the leaf and
run home. Laurie was clearly expecting me to do something about this dreadful happening. And I came through
(I hate to admit) in my best "Supermom" style.

I phoned Debbie's mother and said sweetly, "We have
a problem." I explained the whole episode and waited for
her to solve it just as Laurie had waited for me. Sure

enough, she, too, came through.

"Well," she said thoughtfully, "maybe they should split the leaf and each take a half, would be a good idea?"

I pronounced it an excellent idea, suggested it to Laurie and she met Debbie halfway down the block, where they divided the leaf.

Debbie's mother and I congratulated ourselves on a job well done.

What a shame I deprived Laurie of finding her own solution! Not that it did any lasting harm to her little psyche, but I missed a golden opportunity to help her become more confident.

If I had it to do over I would say, "I can see how upset you are, Laurie. Let's talk about it. What do you think you might do?" Giving her a chance to explore the possibilities for herself would have been much more respectful.

She might have said, "I could never speak to Debbie again."

"That's certainly one option," I'd have agreed.

"I could go take a leaf from Debbie's yard."

"You could do that."

"I could tell Debbie's mother on her."

"Yes, you could."

"I could go find another leaf in our yard."

"There are probably quite a few there," I might agree. Finally, when she'd thought up all her options, I would have asked, "Of all those choices, which do you think you might try?"

"Telling her mother."

"And what do you think her mother might do or say?" We would discuss possibilities and I would end the discussion with, "You're really good at finding lots of solutions, Laurie! I'm eager to hear what you decide to do and how it all comes out. Keep me posted."

That would have been very respectful to all concerned. Instead I "stunted her growth" by moving in at once with a ready-made solution. And that's just one example out of hundreds I look back on and regret. I solved and suggested and rescued four kids several times a day for years and years. It's amazing they turned out so well in spite of me.

I would have been the first to argue with anybody who said I wasn't respecting my children in the days when I overprotected. I *thought* I was being a terrific mother, but actually I was only indulging myself in feeling so necessary to them.

Every time we do something for a child that he could do for himself, we diminish him a little. We rob him of the pleasure of accomplishment and pride he can enjoy as he builds his self-esteem.

In our defense, we do it with the best intentions, not realizing all the things our children can do for themselves. We get so used to doing things for them, we don't think of how much they can do for themselves.

When Lisa was in kindergarten I picked her up with her friend Erin and went to visit Erin's mother. Erin asked Lisa, "Do you want some toast?"

Lisa nodded agreeably, and I watched with amazement as Erin dragged a chair to the kitchen counter and put bread into the toaster. I had never occurred to me that five-year-olds could make toast! I probably would have continued making my children's toast till they were 35 years old, but for that insightful day. Erin had three older brothers, so her mother had already discovered that kids can do all kinds of things.

Most of us do things for our children that are totally unnecessary. I recommend to clients that they let their children start doing their own laundry at age eight. They often look as surprised as I would have, had anyone suggested that to me when my kids were young.

We overlook the fact that today's children can quickly learn how to operate VCRs and computers. Certainly washers and dryers are a lot simpler.

We can begin preparing them when they're five or six. "Sweetie, when you're eight you'll get to do your own laundry!" We say it with the same excitement we'd use in telling them, "When you get a little older you can go visit Grandma and Grandpa all by yourself." And on their eighth birthday, we teach them how to work the washer. We count on some mistakes, but we can anticipate what those might be. So we teach them not to overload, and we explain sorting light and dark colors.

Larry and I used to be head residents in a college men's dormitory. Every September there would be knocks on our door from disturbed young men holding pink shirts and shorts. "Mrs. Schnebly, I washed my clothes and my red socks must have faded on my white stuff. What do I do now?" The poor dears had been deprived of that information at age eight and now had to learn the hard way.

We can do our children a real service by helping them become capable and self-sufficient from the earliest possible age.

While that also frees us parents to spend more time pursuing our own interests, we're often uncomfortable with it. Mothers, especially, get a great deal of satisfaction from being needed, and also from nurturing. Sometimes there is even an unrealized anxiety that our children might not "need" us. Or we may fear their disapproval. We're so vulnerable to their expressions of sadness or fear or anger that we're putty in their hands.

I don't for a moment accuse them of consciously manipulating us, but unconsciously they come to know what they can get away with. Later on in life they often look back and see clearly how they manipulated us. They laugh and shake their heads at how creatively they got their needs and wants met.

But can we, as parents, see the dynamics as clearly while they're happening? I don't think we can because we're too emotionally involved. We see the mistakes easily in *other* families, however. We see a child "abuse" a parent in the supermarket, begging for candy or toys, crying, having temper tantrums, and we see the embarrassed parent writhe in a no-win situation. If the father yells at the tot or slaps him for misbehaving, he risks the disapproval of us observers. If he gives in and buys the child the candy or toy, he still risks the disapproval of us observers.

The kid knows he has Dad over a barrel. That would probably never happen if we had a neighbor's child at the market. Both the neighbor's kid and we would have more respect for one another than to let that situation occur.

If the child said, "Can I have a candy bar?" our response would be a kind, firm, "No." We would see things clearly. Candy is not good for this child and it will not become an issue.

Our enormous love for our own children makes us want them to enjoy pain-free living, which seems to translate into never being deprived. It's as if love clouds respect. I can easily refuse the neighbor's kid whom I *don't* love because I'm clear about what he can or can't "stand." We respect the neighbor kid's ability to handle a candy-less tummy. Our own little angels make us doubt their ability to handle *anything* displeasing to them.

Again, I don't want to sound like I see children as crafty, cunning, selfish individuals who are out to get us. But I do see them as incredibly brilliant in getting their wants met. God gave all of us an innate ability to figure out how to survive, and a precious gift it is! The smarter we are, the better we're able to use that gift to help us get what we want.

It helps to look at our children's manipulative techniques as evidence of their natural intelligence. Instead of being annoyed with them, we can be genuinely grateful they're so smart and capable of figuring things out. Once we think along those lines we'll be able to react logically, instead of emotionally, to their behavior.

Our son Lindsay is now a strapping young man who's independent, and into running and biking. He eats healthy foods and loves Ann. At 27 he looks back with amusement at his early years and gave me permission to use him as an example of children's manipulation and parents' confusion.

He'd been preceded by two older sisters who seemed to him to get all the attention. They already had life made. He, on the other hand, was timid and anxious. He was reluctant to go to friends' houses to play, preferring they come to him. He was afraid of all kinds of things: bees, cement trucks, helicopters and so on. He'd run crying into the house if a loud plane went over and I'd hug him and reassure him.

He was nervous about starting kindergarten, so I drove him every day and was conscientious about driving him home. He was scared to go into his room at night, afraid of the dark and fearful of nightmares, so Larry and I did a lot of reassuring and comforting him. In first grade he couldn't help but love Mrs. Hunt, his teacher. But when the class had a substitute he ran off into the desert. I got a call from the principal's office asking me to come and help find him.

Because he was obviously so afraid of the substitute, I

let him stay home for a few days while she was there. When it was time to return to school, he had developed a full-blown school phobia. He seemed actually in a state of panic before school every morning. I would try to cheer him up, think of fun things to tell him, suggest that "Maybe today you'll get to paint," or anything that might sound positive. I'd drive him to school and pick him up, and encourage him to have friends over. The fears persisted.

By the time he was eight I was exhausted. I was discouraged at not having been able to help him. We took him to the Child Guidance Center, sure they were going to define his condition as a serious mental illness.

The counselor spent a half hour with Lindsay, then a half hour with us before he gave us the feared diagnosis:

"Lindsay discovered very early in life that the best way to get attention in your house was to be afraid. He no doubt stumbled on it accidentally when he felt anxious about something and you immediately overreacted. He got a lot of mileage from his fears . . . they made him special. He couldn't compete with his sisters, so he found something in which he could shine: being scared. As soon as you quit responding to that behavior it will stop."

I was dumbfounded.

Prepared to hear that my son had a rare and incurable emotional illness, I now felt a smoldering resentment, as if I'd been duped. At the same time I felt an enormous relief, and was willing to take the counselor's advice and see what happened.

"Don't be available in the morning for Lindsay to cry to," he said. "Lock yourself in the bathroom and stay there till he's left for school." The counselor explained to Lindsay, as well, that we'd been acting as if Lindsay weren't able to take care of himself, and the counselor knew we were wrong.

We were to stop overprotecting and start encouraging his innate ability to handle his life. Instead of walking with him into his dark room at bedtime, we would say, "Linds, you can do this all by yourself now. We'll stay in the living room and you yell at us when you get as far as the bathroom. Then when you get past the girls' door, and finally when you get your own light turned on." When he arrived there triumphantly we'd all hoot in celebration.

It was a matter of changing focus from rescuing him from his fears to encouraging his ability and "selling" him on our belief in him.

It worked!

"Now you can ride your bike to school like the other kids do," replaced my driving him. The first three mornings he cried outside the bathroom, where I stood wringing my hands in private apprehension, but then he got on his bike and rode to school. After that there were no more attempts at the morning "downers."

The results were so dramatic I found it hard to believe we'd been so long in struggling with a problem that was this easy to solve, once we understood the dynamics.

Lindsay went on a couple of years later to spend a week at Outward Bound, a camp in the mountains in which the final 24 hours were spent completely alone. He came home swaggeringly confident.

Now he hosts a local TV show, and it's occurred to me as I watch with maternal pride that I'm grateful for the counselor who identified the problem. But for him, I'd probably still be driving Lindsay to work every day!

I look back and realize that I lacked respect for Lindsay. I didn't know he was "as capable as" the other kids his age, and thought he needed to be treated with "special handling." He'd have been a dummy *not* to continue along the path that got so much attention showered on him.

Our children are not dummies. They're downright brilliant. So, if we can figure out their "payoffs" for certain behavior, we'll know better how to respond.

If I had it to do over again, I would have been calmly reassuring when Lindsay was frightened at something, but kept a steady confidence within myself that he could handle anything other children could handle. A good measuring stick is other kids' behavior. If everybody else walks to school, your child probably can, too. If all the kids are afraid of a teacher, maybe there's something to investigate.

We can understand our children's desire for special attention and we must make sure they get it for things we want to encourage. Making a big deal over any behavior, positive or negative, is a sure way to make it continue.

Be unimpressed with any behavior you want to discourage. Being unimpressed is slightly different from "ignoring." To ignore something we have to pretend it isn't happening. To be unimpressed, we can be aware of it but just not respond to it. We treat it the way we would an airplane flying over. We may notice it, but we don't pay any special attention to it.

When we quit paying attention to certain behaviors our children exhibit, however, an interesting thing may happen. They may begin to think we don't love them anymore. Sometimes their claim to fame has been so wrapped up in getting attention for a certain activity that they mistake our withdrawal for disinterest. Frequently they will escalate the bad behavior, trying harder and harder to get us involved, and they become even more discouraged when they get no results.

So, while we should turn our attention away from misbehavior—which includes anything we don't want to happen, from acting wild to excessive shyness, persistent fears, refusing to join in, pouting or brooding—it's extremely important to give extra attention for other things at the same time. This is the time to lavish encouragement on the child for anything at all that's positive.

I have a whole chapter on encouragement in my book *Out Of Apples,* so I won't spend much time on it here, except to say encouragement can help us thrive and bloom. Children need encouragement like plants need water, and they wilt drastically when they're deprived of it.

What we should do is notice the child in all kinds of other ways than just for misbehavior. To give her a hug as we pass the breakfast bar where she's having cereal is to say, "Hey, sweetie, I like you."

A pat on the shoulder or a little hand squeeze as we walk to the car together is reassuring. Putting up drawings on the refrigerator and pointing them out with pride to neighbors or other family members is great. Asking advice is a wonderful encourager! "Matthew, do you think I should buy these petunias or these marigolds for our garden?" "Which tablecloth should I use for dinner when the Barkleys come over?" Any comments or questions that show our respect for an individual act as encouragement. We *value* these little people and we want them to know it! So the more we recognize their "goodness," the less we'll have to deal with their "badness."

Each of us has a strong desire to be accepted and respected. We want desperately to belong and to feel important. As parents we have the chance to give our children this crucial self-image.

Marriages are often troubled by differences in beliefs about how children should be handled. A frequent complaint I hear is this:

"My wife is so permissive she's ruining our kids. She

lets them run all over her. They are completely spoiled, and she can't control them. When I'm alone with them they behave just fine, but the minute she comes in the door they start fighting or whining or getting in trouble, somehow. They're constantly demanding things. It's gotten so I hate to go home, there's such turmoil there. She complains how exhausted they make her, but she doesn't discipline them. They abuse her, and she puts up with it. It's going to ruin our marriage."

You can imagine that the father, in his frustration, begins to overreact in the other direction. He becomes the stern, hostile parent, because he knows the kids need to be taught discipline and he thinks he has to balance his wife's permissiveness.

The further she leans toward being too soft, the further he leans toward being too hard. It doesn't do any favors for the kids, but it doesn't seem to harm them as much as it does their parents' relationship. Children have tremendous skills in sizing up how they can behave around each parent, and they act accordingly.

Actually they often enjoy experimenting with their behavior, seeing how far they can go with each parent, with grandparents or sitters. They love a sense of power just as adults do. They'll exercise their power in whatever way they're most successful. The best child, the best-at-being-the-worst child, the most outgoing, the shyest, the healthiest, the sickest, the happiest, the saddest, "our little worrier," "our helper," are all tried-and-true roles.

And all children delight in getting their parents involved with them, whatever it takes. Indeed, they often cooperate to get their parents' attention by fighting with each other.

When things are a bit dull, one or the other will deliberately provoke a scene. Even the tiniest tot learns to knock over his big brother's blocks, so big brother will wail and perhaps clobber the baby as both of them yell and begin their mental countdown: ten, nine, eight, seven, six, five, four, three, two, one . . . here comes Mommy!

Sure enough, there she is, coming in from the kitchen, looking disturbed and saying, "*Now* what is it?" The kids are tickled pink. It worked again!

They've just seen once more that the best way to get attention from Mom is to stage a fight. Even if the attention consists of a lecture or punishment, it's well worth the price to experience that sense of power at getting adults involved.

We should be thrilled with their persistence, even while we determine to defeat their negative methods. We should beam proudly and think, "What fertile little minds they have!" But we'll remember not to get hooked into their game of "Getting Parents Involved."

So we look for ways to encourage their self-reliance. "I notice you two solved your own quarrel. You're getting really good at that! I'm impressed. How about playing a game with me, anybody want to?"

Ideally we'd keep in mind pictures of how we want our children to be as adults, and all our behavior would be working toward that image. Are we fostering their ability to entertain themselves? Are we teaching them our values? Do we rescue them or let them experience the consequences of their actions? Do we respect them? Do we respect *ourselves?* Do we communicate feelings, thoughts, ideas and ordinary day-to-day stories of incidents? Do we show love? How loving are we as wife and husband, and are there signs of affection between us that demonstrate that love to them?

What if we fail in any of these areas? We do and we

will, but that's okay, too, because it's modeling the realities of life. Few of us grew up in homes where the atmosphere was ideal. It might be safe to say that most of us grew up in families where people didn't express their true feelings. There was deceit and disrespect, or criticism instead of encouragement. Throughout all of it the family members put on a show of normalcy that they knew didn't exist.

But that's all right. It didn't kill us, and we always have the opportunity to learn new ideas and beliefs and behavior as we grow up. Certainly it would be a lot easier to grow up in a home where there is always respect, honesty, communication, affection and encouragement, but when there isn't we can either be defeated by it or we can grow from it—*we* decide.

So, if we make mistakes as parents, we needn't spend much time harboring our regrets. Don't say, "If only." Say, "Next time." Indeed, if we were perfect parents, perhaps our children would be cheated out of the opportunity to learn from our mistakes. And though we'd prefer *not* being unfair or disrespectful, our kids may become a little tougher by experiencing *some* unfair treatment now and then.

There are always going to be teachers, neighbors, bosses, friends and spouses who treat them unfairly. Life is not fair. Perhaps they would be too tender and vulnerable if they had never experienced that at home.

So we mustn't be too hard on ourselves for our imperfections in parenting. Let's chalk them up as reminders that people are prone to making mistakes; our children are entitled to make them as well.

It's wonderful when we can readily admit our mistakes to our children. To prove that we have all the answers is not necessary. To show we're always seeking to learn is exemplary. To apologize to them for our angry outbursts or other behavior we regret is marvelous modeling. We don't have to always be right. We can say, "I don't know," and "Maybe I'm wrong." We can ask, "What do *you* think?" to our four-year-olds or our teenagers.

As parents we needn't be perfect, thank goodness; but we do have to be the family leaders. We're not here to fulfill their every need or desire. We're the camp directors, trying to help our charges learn, grow and expand their horizons.

Chapter 13

Marrying the Family

In-laws. The very word sounds ominous. More jokes have been told about in-laws than almost anybody else. (Someone said that we laugh at the things we're afraid of.)

I could almost entitle this chapter "Fear" because that's what it's all about. But it's encouraging to realize that many of our problems stem from fear. Knowing that takes some of the sting out of the pain and gives us a direction to work toward alleviating the fear rather than building up walls of protection.

I wonder how many wars have been fought out of fear, and how many could have been avoided if the people involved had been able to talk about their fears instead of becoming enemies.

Alfred Adler taught that man's greatest need is the need to belong. We all hunger for the security of being loved and accepted and thought worthwhile. Most of us feel that acceptance in our original families, but it begins to be threatened when we branch out and start new families.

We're astonished when the dreaded in-law syndrome settles on *us,* because we never thought of ourselves as mean or selfish or controlling or rigid or domineering, or any of the nasty words associated with in-laws. We're caring and thoughtful and considerate! To know us is to love us. Everybody *else* likes us. How is it that only the new mother-in-law, father-in-law, son-in-law or daughter-in-law objects to us? We feel victimized, thrown into a role we didn't want.

Most of us rooted for Romeo and Juliet, and loathed their closed-minded families for trying to prevent their marriage. Our hearts went out to Maria and Tony in *West Side Story* as they fought against the prejudices of their extended families. We are a culture that believes in falling in love and choosing our lifelong partners ourselves.

And so everyone says sensible things like, "Whomever my children choose for their spouses I will love. I want only for them to be happy." And everyone means it. What goes wrong, then? Why is there so much pain involved with the families we marry?

Fear.

We fear change. We fear the unknown. We fear not being loved and accepted for who we are. We fear being expected to love someone we don't know very well, yet. What if they aren't the kind of people we're drawn to? What if they have entirely different beliefs? What if they alienate this treasured loved one of mine and I lose him or her forever?

Both sides are sharing the same fears. When we fear anything we tend to want to escape from it. That's an innate protective habit. Run. Avoid. Shut out.

And in the case of in-laws, that's the direct opposite of what we should do.

We can become so terrified we lose all confidence and begin to act differently around The Person than we do around anyone else. We're frozen into a false kind of manner; a kind of phony smile through teeth clenched in fright, trying to act as if we're comfortable when inside we're scared to death.

If one of us would say, "I'm scared of you," maybe the other would make the same admission, because that's basically all that's wrong with any of us.

We can understand fear because we've experienced it in so many other areas. Perhaps we've learned to handle our fear of flying, of dogs, heights or snakes, but we haven't been able to practice dealing with this fear until we find ourselves in the thick of it; cornered, sweating and feeling helpless.

As a little girl I picked up on the strained relationship between my mother and her mother-in-law. It seemed to me that Grandma just didn't like Mama. My interpretation was that mothers-in-law were to be feared, because if they didn't like you, you were in for a life of trouble.

When I married Larry I approached my in-laws with timid trepidation. I laugh now when I remember writing them a letter and copying it three times to assure that it was perfect so they wouldn't disapprove of me. Years later when I confessed that to Lucille, my mother-in-law, she looked at me with amazement as well as amusement and said, "You *did?*"

She knew I had nothing to fear from her, but I'd been aware of their discomfort about Larry marrying a Catholic. (It's funny to look back at how many times religions have gotten traded back and forth. God must be amused as He watches the big flap it causes sometimes, when in the next generation everybody is going to be switching again. I doubt that He gets too concerned.)

But I came to be very fond of my mother-in-law and she of me. Over the years I watched various friends and relatives struggle with their new in-laws. I would puzzle over all the resentments and hostilities. I'd begun to see in-law discomfort as the norm rather than the exception.

And it continues. Almost every week in my counseling office I hear statements from tense clients: "My mother-in-law wanted her son to marry someone with a college degree. She didn't approve of me because I was a waitress. It took years before she accepted me."

"I told my son-in-law that if he ever so much as makes my daughter cry, I'm going to tear him limb from limb. She's still my little girl and I have to protect her."

"My daughter-in-law forbids me to give my grandchildren even one cookie. She believes sugar is bad for them, and I can't have the pleasure of seeing them enjoy my cookies." (The counterpart: "My daughter-in-law stuffs my grandchild with sweets and I can hardly stand it. It's all I can do to keep my mouth shut.")

"My father-in-law lords it over us with money. He buys us things; TV sets and even cars, and I resent it. He acts like I can't support his daughter. I don't want his money, and I wish he'd butt out of our life."

In every comment runs a common thread: fear. Everyone's afraid of changes they're expected to make; of having to give up behavior or values that are important and precious to them. We're scared of not being loved anymore, of being rejected, or of just not feeling like we belong.

It would be lovely if we didn't have to endure this strained stage. Some few lucky ducks escape it, usually when they've known each other for a long time and have had time to get used to each other. But the majority of us seem to experience it for some period of time . . . perhaps like an initiation.

It helps to know that this strain is common; we're not the only ones enduring it. Most of us get over it. We simply have to know that there are tried-and-true ways to handle fear of any kind.

The best way is to make ourselves *do the thing we fear to do,* and before long we've licked it. If we're afraid of heights we have to go over bridges. Afraid to fly? Take some airplane trips. Dogs? Get one for a pet.

The problem only worsens when we back away from what we fear, yet that is our tendency. The more we distance ourselves, the more afraid and estranged we become.

When our son Lyle met Ginger, we were eager to meet her because we could tell she was special to him. We got to join them for brunch, and were delighted with her openness and sense of humor. She was the picture of confidence and easiness, and we couldn't help seeing how well they "matched."

There was no surprise when Lyle confided that he thought they might get married someday. I told him honestly I thought they had a genuinely good relationship.

In just a few months, however, they were setting a wedding date. I then began to feel apprehensive. It seemed to me they were rushing into a decision that was too important to make so quickly. So, one day when we were having a lighthearted lunch, I told them my thoughts.

"I know I'm biased," I admitted, "because I spend so much of every day hearing stories of married people who are unhappy. Most of them *thought* they were perfectly suited to each other, but now after some years together they have lots of problems stemming from the differences they are now able to see.

"I think you two are rushing into this," I continued, "and I feel like I have to tell you my feelings. But if you still go ahead with your plans I promise I'll support you a hundred percent. I'm not trying to talk you out of marrying . . . only into waiting a little longer."

Both Lyle and Ginger *looked* receptive and composed and as friendly and warm as ever, but I'd shaken Ginger to the core. From then on our relationship changed. She drew back in hurt, feeling I was rejecting her, and I drew back in fear that now I had alienated them for good.

We still interacted, but there was a sense of apprehension and anxiety that made family festivities hardly festive. Birthdays and special occasions that used to be full of warmth and laughter were now feeble attempts at trying to act like we were having a good time, when underneath we all felt the strain.

Ginger felt uncomfortable and confided in Lyle. I felt uncomfortable and confided in Lyle. Lyle was in the worst position of all, loving all the people involved, yet helpless to foster any sense of genuine warmth among us.

But we proceeded diligently, perhaps courageously, with the wedding plans. Both families seemed to enjoy the actual wedding and reception; and I really think we all did, because we had decided to. It was going to happen, and we wanted it to be happy and special for the bride and groom.

All of us hoped that somehow down the road, things would smooth out. And we knew that we had one strong thread in common—we loved Lyle. We *wanted* to be comfortable and close to one another.

One day I decided to make an audio tape, because I felt I could tell Ginger what I was thinking in a slow, safe, carefully thought-out way. I sat down one morning and talked to her the most honestly I ever had, describing my fears, hurts and hopes; all into my safe little tape recorder microphone. I shed a tear here and there, and it was very therapeutic for me to get all of those thoughts expressed. I dropped the tape at their house for them to listen to at their leisure. It seemed to help immeasurably. They listened to it together, and Lyle called to say thanks. Ginger wrote me a note saying she thought we could forget the past hurts and start all over, because she wanted to as much as I did.

We agreed that with the desire we had to mend fences and be close, we could certainly achieve a good relationship. We're both smart, sensitive to others' feelings and able to do what we set out to do. When we have a common goal, such as feeling comfortable together, there is nothing to stop us.

Lyle and Ginger have been married two years now, and it's a tribute to both Ginger and me that I'm able to write this. Our comfort level with each other is good enough so we can expose this very personal account about a situation that once seemed so threatening I would not have thought this chapter possible.

We still don't have the closeness we feel with our *own* families, but that should keep improving if we keep communicating. Intimacy develops as we spend time with each other and share experiences. Every family vacation, indeed every shared experience of any kind, helps form the bonds that encourage closeness and comfort.

There's no hurry. We have a lifetime ahead of us to deepen our relationship. It will ripen naturally if we let it, accepting the newness and the discomfort as normal and temporary. Any good relationship takes time and effort. If we don't pressure ourselves, we may come to love each other genuinely.

I'm not sure anyone ever feels the same closeness to in-laws that we feel with our own original families. There's nothing wrong with that. There's a special bond between parents and their children that is seldom matched, although in some cases it does develop. The toughest relationship seems to be between mother-in-law and daughter-in-law. Young men generally have an easier time fitting in with their wives' families than young women do their husbands'. Men are *supposed* to "leave their families and cleave to their wives," and women stay closer to their families all their lives.

The fact that women do stay closer to their families helps those families feel less threatened by the new groom in their lives. The man's family, on the other hand, frequently feels shut out when he abruptly disappears with his bride. They miss sharing his life. It doesn't occur to a lot of men to call Mom and say hello, while women call home all the time. It would probably help everyone adjust more quickly if both the bride and groom kept up a caring intimacy with their own families, as well as with their in-laws.

The best thing we can do for ourselves and each other is to expect that naturally, our child-in-law will love his or her own family the most, and that gradually we'll all become closer anyway . . . by gentle exposure. All we need to do is treat our in-laws like *friends,* rather than like family. With friends we're usually comfortable and easy and far less emotionally involved than we are with family.

Maybe that's good. Perhaps it wouldn't hurt us a bit to treat our own children more like friends than like family.

I would never go to a friend's home and say, "Cherie, you should trim back your philodendrons; they're looking rangy." Alas, I confess I've said that very thing to Lisa.

Would I ever tell a friend, "Barbara, don't you think you need a haircut?" Of course not. But I say it to Laurie without much hesitation. It's hard for us mothers to keep our mouths shut because we get so used to telling our kids what we think they should do.

So, maybe that little distance between parents and

kids-in-law is healthy. Certainly it's respectful to give them credit for being able to make their own decisions; respect we often don't give our own children.

In dealing with in-laws, it's important to maintain a sense of respect, but with clear and honest communication.

My friend Ann said the biggest problem in her marriage was the lack of support and understanding she got from her husband, especially when it came to her feelings about his parents. He acted as if all her complaints were just her imagination, and refused to give them any importance at all.

That left her in a terribly uncomfortable position of aloneness, experiencing rejection from his family and being unable to find comfort from the most important person in her life. She found herself in a no-win position of disapproval from all sides; first her in-laws, then her husband if she looked to him for support. Of course she became more and more fearful.

The problem escalated when their daughter was born. Gertie, her mother-in-law, immediately stepped in and "took charge." She would constantly ignore Ann's wishes regarding the child's behavior. If Ann said, "Don't run in the house," Gertie would quickly tell the little girl, "It's okay to run in the house, dear." Ann felt more and more like a "non-person," whose thoughts and words were meaningless.

Eventually the marriage ended in divorce, and Ann looks back on the in-law situation as the chief cause.

She and I have talked about how she might have handled things differently if she'd been wiser in those days. "I never really confronted Gertie with what she was doing," Ann reflected. "I felt like *she* knew exactly what she was doing and chose to do it anyway, so talking about it wouldn't do any good. When I tried to tell my husband he just cut me off as imagining things. If I were giving advice to someone in that same position, I'd say she should talk about it. A lot!"

I suspect a marriage counselor could have been helpful. Had Ann's self-esteem been a little better she would have felt more justified in asserting herself, not letting herself be railroaded into submission. But she was too discouraged even to *want* to save the marriage after a few years of living with the noncommunicative, unsupportive husband, so she let the whole thing go.

An assertive wife might have said firmly to Gertie, "We have a problem. When you override my orders to Sally, I feel hurt because you act like I don't exist. Then I become angry because I feel you have no respect for me. I'm not willing to bring Sally to visit or even come myself unless we get this straightened out."

You can be sure Gertie would reconsider very quickly if it meant losing the company of the precious grandchild. And she should. She had the right to rear her own children however she chose, but Ann had the same right.

I think Ann's husband was insensitive in not caring about her complaints, but I don't think he should have jumped in as the rescuer. We make a mistake in thinking the "loved one in common" should get everyone in harmony, because that's an impossible task for anyone. It's easy to see why we fall into that trap . . . we're afraid to make waves with the in-laws, so we prefer someone else doing it for us. Even if that person were willing and able to do it, however, we'd be stunting our own growth. It's good for us to settle our own disputes.

I would have urged Ann's husband, however, to spend a lot of time listening to Ann, understanding her feelings and discussing her options with her. He might have said,

"Honey, I feel badly that Mom makes you feel this way. I love you, and I don't want to see anyone hurt you. You know I'm behind you a hundred percent. You have my permission to tell anyone in my family how you feel about anything they do. I would want them to do the same with you. And I'll be happy to talk about your problems with you anytime you want."

That's the ideal, in my opinion, but few mates are that sensitive and/or skilled in relationship communication. If Ann's husband had been, they would probably still be married.

Perhaps, then, their biggest problem was not in-laws, per se, but the lack of closeness between them because of his lack of sensitivity.

There are many times when we're not sure where our responsibilities lie. If we're even halfway compassionate people, we hurt when we see someone we love hurting. Our tendency often is to jump in and help, whatever that may entail. But when we do that we may only fan the fire and worsen an already uncomfortable situation.

Let's say a bride is put off by her father-in-law's manner. She complains to her husband, and she looks for sympathy as well from her own parents, brothers and sisters. The groom feels terrible that his bride is uncomfortable, so he has a talk with his mother about what to do. Mom sympathizes, but she takes her husband's side and confides in their two daughters and son-in-law, all of whom resent the bride's selfishness. Bride, meanwhile, is getting pretty hostile with dad-in-law. She's going for more and more understanding to her own brothers, sister and sister-in-law. Now, the sisters-in-law are strained in their relationship with the parents-in-law. The bride resents her brother-in-law's wife butting in and the groom's father is turning to the son's sister-in-law and her father. And if this doesn't make any sense to you don't feel bad. I lost track somewhere in the first few sentences. But it shows the dynamics of "too many cooks" helping spoil a relationship; a common phenomenon that's almost the norm.

Everybody becomes a marriage counselor, giving advice to the bride and groom, and then they often become psychiatrists, analyzing the interaction of the entire extended family.

"Julie is paranoid. She thinks we spend all our time talking about her. Ha! I think that's called 'grandiosity.' Who does she think she is that we spend all our time thinking about her?"

"The one I'm worried about is Marvin. I think he's neurotic . . . he never wants to do what the rest of us are doing. He's becoming a recluse."

"He says he just can't stand Melanie's attitude. He says she's manic depressive, and he can't put up with her mood swings."

"She can't help that; she's an adult child of an alcoholic and grew up in a dysfunctional family. You notice how Melanie's always eating? That's because she's overly sensitive and can't assert herself. She needs to get help."

"What she needs is to divorce Mark. He is so totally irresponsible. All he has going for him are his looks. He's narcissistic."

And so on. We all do it. Usually it's harmless, but it can get out of hand if people take themselves too seriously. They may begin to "choose up sides" and end up with gangs like the Jets and the Sharks, resulting in rumbles and wars at family Christmas dinners.

If you find yourself dreading the Fourth of July family picnic, know that you're not alone. Interacting with one's own family can often be difficult. And when you get a bunch of in-laws with *their* in-laws as well, you've got "trouble in River City."

The trick is to brainwash ourselves by saying over and over, "Live and let live." We have a responsibility to live our own lives as well as we can, and that takes plenty of energy. There's no need to try to live each other's as well . . . let them handle their own.

We can watch all their family dramas with interest, as we do soap operas or situation comedies, but we don't have to get involved with the emotional involvement any more than we would a TV show. We can be pleasant, respectful observers.

Sometimes, of course, there is just no hope of achieving a good relationship with in-laws. In rare situations you marry into a family who are so swamped with pain and problems that they're absolutely miserable individuals. You may try to be nice, considerate, open, pleasing, thoughtful, and every other positive trait you can conjure up. Still you face nonacceptance and rejection.

You try to communicate respectfully. You pull out your best listening skills. You say "When you . . . I feel . . . because . . . ." sentences. You invite them over for dinner. You get only hostility in return.

Eventually you may decide to stop trying, because you're dealing with people who have been hurt so deeply and are carrying around such enormous loads of pain they're looking for someone to blame—you're a handy target. At some point, in a case like that, retreat.

Retreating is not the same as rejecting. It isn't punishing with hostile coolness. It's simply giving the other party or parties the space they seem to want, not imposing your company on them, and yet, being as cordial as you would be toward any acquaintance.

Each of us gets to decide what we will do in any circumstance. For instance, Ann might have said to her mother-in-law, "Gertie, I'll be happy to come to Thanksgiving dinner, but if you overrule my instructions to Sally we'll leave."

Then Ann *will* leave when she's undermined, pleasantly but promptly. "Bye everybody . . . see you soon. Dinner was great, Gertie. C'mon, Sally." Her husband may stay or leave, that's his choice. Ann is taking care of her needs.

We wouldn't be happy doing that kind of thing if it were selfish or unfair . . . only after we've given the matter plenty of thought and have come to terms with what is fair and respectful to both parties.

But this is a last resort. Usually we don't have to go that far to get along with our in-laws. Most of them are just like *us,* wanting a good relationship and wondering how to achieve it.

Here's my best advice in being (and dealing with) an in-law:

1. Lower expectations of yourself. Don't beat yourself up if you're not immediately enthralled with your in-laws. Quit feeling like you "should" love them. (As Albert Ellis says, "Don't *should* on yourself.") And give them the same permission not to be crazy about you.

2. Accept the fact that you're different from one another. You each have a lifetime of different experiences, different ancestry, different belief systems, different likes and dislikes and different goals. Perhaps the only thing you have in common is the person you love. Don't feel guilty that you're not alike. It's good for families to get "new blood" and our ways tend to rub off on each other. Look at the differences as fresh viewpoints, but not as barriers you have to overcome or change.

You both have the right to stay exactly the way you are if you so choose.

3. Recognize the problem between you as *fear*. It's much less threatening when you can see through the apparent hostility and find the scared child underneath. Know that no matter how old the cold, defensive person may be, he or she is still a scared child when it comes to in-law relationships.

4. Don't be dishonest, but temper honesty with kindness. An honest relationship doesn't mean brutal frankness, which can be very hurtful. It does mean plenty of conversation and describing of feelings.

5. Mutual respect must *always* be present. Not only do you need to respect your in-laws, but you absolutely must respect yourself as well. If you always consider their wishes and feelings while ignoring your own, you're going to build up enormous resentment that will inevitably be destructive. Admittedly, it's tough to decide where the balance is as you try to respect both parties, but it's essential to respect both yourself and your in-laws.

6. Consider all the in-laws as friends. Friendships develop quickly or slowly, deeply or shallowly, but any of them can enhance our lives if we allow them to go at their own pace.

7. Don't look to your mate to solve your problems for you. Nor should you feel responsible for being the go-between for your spouse and your family. Do, however, make sure all the people concerned know they have your permission to discuss their concerns with the appropriate parties. Be attentive and interested, and lovingly encourage them to *do* something about their problems. You don't have to take sides. Certainly, if someone's actions are affecting your life, you, too, have the right to talk to that person about it. But the kindest thing you can do is to involve yourself in your mate's feelings and leave the actual solving to him or her.

Who's Responsible?

W hen you were a little kid who washed the windows in your house, Mom or Dad? Who put gas in the car? Who did the laundry, the yard work, the painting? Did Dad get up on Sunday morning and make pancakes? Was it Mom's job to trim the Christmas tree?

Whatever you observed in those early days was helping you form your expectations of who does what job in marriage. You learn those "truths" without realizing they're not chiseled in stone, and you proceed into your own marriage, fully expecting the other person to share those same beliefs.

None of us wants to do things we find especially unpleasant, but most of us have decided which responsibilities we're willing to consider taking on.

"I will never clean toilets," Victoria told me firmly. "Daddy did that; it's not women's work."

There's nothing wrong with Victoria's belief about the required sex of toilet cleaners, unless she marries Jake who says firmly, "I'm not about to clean the toilet. I wouldn't even know how; Mother never taught me. A man shouldn't have to clean a toilet."

He, too, has every right to his conviction, but what do they do now? Both firmly believe they're right, and they're not about to consider changing their stances.

So what else is new? Their problem is par for the course and certainly one that's solvable. It requires only mutual respect and the desire to cooperate. (Actually that's true of every aspect of marriage. Perhaps I needn't have written this book at all, but just stated, "A happy marriage requires only mutual respect and the desire to cooperate!")

But maybe I can share some suggestions I've picked up from other couples who have found good ways to promote cooperation.

One method comes from an Episcopalian priest who said, "My wife and I made up a card game. We write down on three-by-five cards all the chores that need to be done. We sit down and take cards we're willing to be responsible for, but both of us understand it's not a permanent assignment. Anytime one of us wants to change jobs we ask for a new game and start to negotiate.

"For instance, last week I told Mary Anne that I was tired of taking out the trash, and I wanted to trade that card for one of hers. She was sick of being responsible for getting baby sitters, and we agreed that was a fair trade. I took the baby sitter card and she took the trash one. We'll live by that until one of us requests another card game, and then we'll trade around again."

"You make it sound wonderfully simple," I said. "Is it always such an easy exchange? What if Mary Anne doesn't want to take out trash?"

"Sometimes it takes a lot of finagling," he admitted. "Sometimes we sit there for hours trying to agree on what's fair; but we always do eventually, maybe out of sheer exhaustion. We've gotten good at negotiating. One of us might say, 'I'll trade cleaning up the dog poop for paying the bills.' The other might say, 'No way. I enjoy writing checks, but I loathe cleaning up dog poop.' Maybe it might take two jobs to replace one, like, 'I'll pay the bills and keep the cars gassed up if you'll agree to pick up after Poochie.'"

Any arrangement is fine, as long as both people agree on it. The division of labor shouldn't ever be permanently defined, in my opinion, unless both people happen to love their job responsibilities and have no desire to change. I liked George and Mary Anne's creative solution as much as they did.

The only time it wouldn't be successful, it seems, is if one or both parties lost the desire to cooperate and made the whole thing a power struggle. I could see either spouse refusing to give up a card or setting the exchange so high the other couldn't comply. Because power struggles never solve a problem, when one occurs, it must be recognized and dealt with for cooperation to resume.

"I'm discouraged. We've been sitting here for two hours and nothing I suggest will let me get rid of the window-washing job. You seem determined not to take that over no matter how much I offer to do in exchange. And I'm sick of washing windows. What do you suggest?" Asking for suggestions often creates an atmosphere of respect that begins to inspire actual problem solving. Instead of tenaciously refusing to cooperate, the uncooperative partner may begin to think of new solutions.

"Maybe we should hire a window-washing service." Or, "Could we pay the kid across the street to do it?" Or even, "Windows just get dirty again; why wash them at all?"

For the most part we seem more willing to do the jobs that fit with our picture of how life should be. Having a clean house is more my priority than Larry's, so I'm more willing to make it happen. But I'm certainly not going to be responsible for all of it, nor would he expect me to be.

It doesn't seem fair that one person take more responsibility for household chores than the other. Nor is it necessarily fair that one be more responsible for earning money than the other. It all boils down to a division of labor in which both parties are equally responsible for the good of the family unit.

Traditionally men hunted the animals and women cooked them. Some of us still like our roles defined exactly that way. Many men are the breadwinners and women the homemakers. That's perfect when both like that arrangement.

But more and more women find a lot of pleasure in working outside the home, as men do, and are contributing sizeable incomes to the running of the home. Men have changed their priorities to allow for more time with the children, and I heartily applaud that attitude.

The best arrangement, as far as I'm concerned, would be letting both Mom and Dad work at an outside job half the time and take care of the house and children the other half. It's good for us to experience what our mates have to do, or *get* to do. (Probably most of us suspect the other person has it easier than we do.) But few of us could get half-time jobs that would make that arrangement feasible, so we have to work within the system we have.

The whole issue of responsibilities will be a constantly changing picture as each of us moves into different ages and roles. So, like George and Mary Anne, we need to expect changes and allow for them.

If we look at each phase as simply a different job description rather than a sentence to hard labor, we can handle it easily. What makes the issue difficult is our belief system that is filled with shoulds and oughts, and expectations that have practically become moral values.

Wouldn't it be great if we could wipe the slate clean and start our marital working arrangement from scratch?

I remember my mother looking at all the bright new towels we got as wedding presents and saying, "How nice that you get to start out with all towels that match!" She had a collection of colors and styles that had accumulated over the years and were still "too good to throw out," so the bathroom displayed a strange and sometimes jarring assortment.

We could look at our expectations and beliefs the same way. We have so many that are old and shabby, but we hang onto them without realizing they could be replaced with new beliefs . . . and it wouldn't even cost the price of new towels! It would cost only our time in conversation.

We'd have to be willing to discard all the shoulds. Our purpose would be to think of all the ways either of us might contribute to the family unit and simply divide them up according to our skills, as well as our preferences.

My daughter Laurie, who edits all my books for me, is a very bright, creative woman who loves her job at an advertising agency. She's never been a homemaker. Turning out a gourmet dinner or polishing the furniture does not fill her heart with joy like creating sparkling copy or producing a successful TV commercial.

Her husband Pete, on the other hand, doesn't find pleasure in a job. Unlike many men whose ego is directly connected to work, Pete is happy running marathons and competing in Scrabble tournaments and "pondering." When their son Christopher was born, they worked out a great arrangement in which Pete was the primary caretaker of the baby and housework while Laurie brought home paychecks. She takes part in Christopher's care, to be sure, and Pete now works as an optician. But until Christopher started preschool, their main jobs were vice versa. It worked very well.

Any arrangement is workable. The hardest part is getting rid of old, stereotyped beliefs.

Our preferences as well as our skills should help determine our delegated chores. Generally, we think of women as the official seamstresses. (I don't even think there's a word for male "seamsters.") One of my female clients has finally put her foot down and announced to her family that they may use the sewing machine anytime they want, but she's given up sewing forever.

Her husband happens to be a very detail-oriented, patient man, good with his hands. He sews on scout badges with invisible stitches.

She's good at painting entire rooms quickly, while he painstakingly does the careful trimming. It finally made sense to them that he is better suited to sewing and mending and she is better suited to mowing the lawn with the power mower.

It makes me wonder how many roles we're stuck in simply by tradition. It might open wonderful new areas of interest when we begin to investigate what we're doing because we want to, and what we're doing because of society's expectations.

Many times my clients are angry at what they see as an unfair division of labor.

Margo said, "I work an eight-hour day at a print shop. Then I come home and clean the house, cook the dinner, take care of the kids' needs, do the laundry, clean up the dishes, make everyone's lunches for the next day, get the kids bathed and in bed, then fall into bed myself, exhausted. James puts in his time at the office and that's it."

Unfair, right? But listen to James.

"Hey, I'm not a jerk. First of all I work a good 10 to 12 hours every day. I have to work that much overtime to pay for the huge new house Margo had to have. I pay for a cleaning lady twice a week. A lot of the time we all eat out; it's not like she cooks many meals. And also I'm willing to do my share of the housework . . . it's just that I don't do it 'right,' which is how Margo thinks it should be done. She thinks none of us does anything right, so she has to do it herself. No wonder she's exhausted. She never rests; but it's sure not my fault, the way she makes it sound."

In this case the problem was Margo's need to be Wonder Woman. Sometimes, though, a husband or wife is *not* putting in an equal share. One of the techniques I suggest as a kind of measuring stick is this:

Put a piece of paper on the kitchen counter or any handy place where you can both jot down time spent on anything you do for the good of the family unit. For a week or two keep track of your times. Then you'll can see in black and white how equally your labor is divided. It's a bit of a nuisance, writing it all down, but it also becomes kind of fun as you watch your efforts get recorded. In fact, sometimes people begin working extra hard so they can prove they're doing the lion's share.

If you work an eight-hour shift someplace, you get to record not only the eight hours, but also your travel time to and from work. Jot down 17 minutes stopping at the grocery store, 38 minutes preparing dinner, 42 minutes bathing kids and reading them their stories, and so on.

On the weekend you get credit for yard work, washing cars, driving kids to soccer practice, anything at all that contributes to the good of the family. Watching TV doesn't count. Somebody asked, "What about reading the paper?

It should count. I'm keeping abreast of what's going on in the world, and then I'm better able to keep the children informed."

I think that's reaching. If we went that far we could excuse almost *any* activity as beneficial to the family. "Getting my hair done makes me feel so much better I'm a nicer wife and mother the whole rest of the day, so I should be allowed to count hairdresser time." I don't think so.

"What about helping the neighbor with his cooler? That's not leisure time. Can't I count that?" No. It's wonderful to help your neighbor, but it doesn't affect your family's well being. Fixing your own cooler certainly counts.

It takes a little time figuring out what you can and can't count, but usually you come to agree on the guidelines. Sometimes it becomes clear that one person really is badly overloaded. Other times both people see that their work is pretty evenly divided. I think it's well worth the small amount of time it takes if you find yourselves arguing about pulling your weight. At least you can both *see* the fairness or unfairness you've been arguing about.

There are no "right and wrong" ways to divvy up the labor; only finding workable plans that are suitable to both people. Like any partnership, marriage is full of shared responsibilities.

Generally speaking, money is power. The person who earns it traditionally had the most power in the relationship. The other person often felt like a second-class citizen, whether or not he or she should.

It's demeaning for anyone to have to ask for money, and yet many non-working spouses get none unless they do. One of my neighbors must ask for the exact amount of money she will need to buy the groceries or give the kids for lunch money. Her husband insists on an accurate accounting of all she spends. Needless to say, she no longer loves him at all. She's staying only until the children are old enough to be on their own. Then she'll be out of there . . . unless they make some changes.

Other marriages work on an allowance basis. Both partners get a certain amount of money they can spend as they please. The amount is exactly the same for both. That's a pretty fair arrangement if both are working equally for the good of the family.

When Laurie and Pete got married they formed a corporation called *Acme Dynamics Ltd.* It exists only in their minds, but it's the "business" that provides the operating expenses for their marriage. They were both earning money and they decided that each of them would put a certain percentage of their income into Acme Dynamics to pay for rent, utilities, food, insurance and other necessities. When Pete quit his job to take care of Christopher, Laurie put her entire income into Acme, which paid them both an equal allowance every month.

It isn't a bad idea to have a "business" within the marriage. Marriage is made up of so many facets, and the business part of it is one we seldom consider beforehand. We somehow think money won't be a problem when we're in love.

In fact, money is a big problem in many marriages. It needn't be if it's discussed and decisions are made jointly in a respectful way. It gets out of proportion when people carry around resentment over unresolved money issues.

Larry and I started out earning nearly equal salaries, but when we had babies we agreed I would quit my job. Even though I was eager to stay home and be a mother, wife and homemaker, I really missed having money I felt was mine, to do whatever I wanted with.

Larry didn't feel like the "powerful one," but I felt he was because our sustenance depended solely on him. Very soon I started teaching piano at home so I could have something to spend as I pleased. That's how we got into the habit we're still into today: his money buys most of our necessities; mine buys non-necessities. We're both comfortable with that. I will happily furnish the entire house with my income, but I'd die before I'd buy a loaf of bread. The arrangement works because we both think it's fine.

We have a difference of opinion on what to do with extra money. He likes to spend his on experiences and I like to spend mine on things.

Actually, it works out well because I get to go on vacations he pays for, and he gets to live in the snazzy new room I fixed up. From time to time we shake our heads in mild disapproval at the other's ways, but we no longer feel *strong* disapproval at each other's peculiarities. He just can't see why I would buy new carpeting when the old is "still good," and I can't imagine his spending that much money for a river raft trip down the Grand Canyon.

But we don't have to have the same values. We just have to respect each other's right to have different ones.

These differences are minor, I realize, compared to people who see their spouse "throwing away money" on alcohol or hobbies, or anything else that takes away from the necessities of life. And this seems to happen fairly often. One party will be a spendthrift while the other has to scrimp to pay for groceries.

That's very unfair, of course, and needs to be dealt with if there's going to be any harmony in the relationship. Sometimes it helps to consult a marriage or financial counselor, a pastor or rabbi, or anyone else who's respected.

Some folks swear by budgets. Some use the envelope

system, where you put so much money in envelopes for rent, clothes, movies, etc. Some prefer to spend it as they get it and suffer the consequences when they run out.

The point I'm making is that almost *nobody* finds finances to be problem free, except maybe the very wealthy. But that's okay. It just means you have to talk and talk and talk as you work out compromises. And sometimes you have to shut up, too. One wife confided that she had argued with her husband for months about some scuba gear he wanted to buy. When she finally backed off and said, "I guess if you can find the money for it, you should go ahead and get it," he said, "I guess I can't really afford it," and that was the end of that.

Which proves that money can often turn into the basis of a power struggle, just like anything else can. Sometimes the actual dollars have less to do with our arguments than does the desire to "win."

It's good to remind ourselves that the family unit is a cooperative venture in which everyone involved pulls his own weight as much as he's able. The man and woman expend energy on a relatively equal basis to take care of their own and the other's needs. As the children grow they lend their energies to caring for *their* own and others' needs. No one except babies and tiny tots (and maybe pets) should get a free ride in life.

It doesn't much matter whether we contribute by baking pies or earning corporate-president salaries, as long as we contribute fairly. Neither partner should feel superior by virtue of his financial capacity; nor should he feel inferior, as long as he's being as productive a member as he's able.

But why is money such a sticky subject in marriage? I think it's symbolic of character in our minds. We don't want to be thought of as "tight," "spendthrift" or "selfish," so we may hesitate to speak up about our feelings. Even if we do express ourselves, we may go along with our partners' wishes rather than risk disapproval. But then we build up resentments that do more harm than if we'd stood our ground in the first place.

I'm thinking of a woman I worked with who had brought a "nice nest egg" of family stocks and bonds into her marriage and had watched it all disappear in a two-year period as her husband invested in high-risk ventures. She had believed in his business expertise at first, but when she became alarmed at how much they'd lost, she still allowed him to use the stocks because she felt "a wife should." Finally, they were reduced to selling their house and renting a small apartment. She was relegated to making hamburgers in a fast-food place, bitter at what her lifestyle had become.

Was it her moral obligation as a wife to make those funds available to her husband for investment? That would be a dandy conversation piece for your next dinner party, because you'd get a lot of strong and varied reactions. Some people would say, "Of course it was. Marriage means both people contribute all they own for the common good."

And some would argue, "It wasn't good sense to lose everything when obviously the man was lacking fiscal skills."

And some would answer, "If she expected to share in the rewards if his investments paid off, she should be willing to share the unsuccessful outcome as well."

It beats me. I tend to believe, however, that both parties should be entitled to keep savings or funds that were family heritages unless, of course, they're needed for food and shelter. Speculation should be done only if one can afford it, and it seems to me the little nest egg should have been held in safety. If I had been that wife, I would probably would have said a kind, firm "No" when my husband asked for the stocks. But as a starry-eyed bride, I probably would have done exactly what she did; given a reluctant "Yes" because I loved my knight in shining armor so much I wouldn't expect problems up ahead.

So, *love* clouds the issue of financial negotiation within marriage, making it difficult to work out wise decisions because they're so emotionally colored.

I know a husband whose wife went through thousands of dollars (his) buying expensive gifts for her family. She explained, "When I love someone I like to show it by buying nice things for them; it's not like we can't afford it."

He was feeling guilty about his resentment, unsure of whether or not he should set some kind of limit, afraid he'd be called a cheapskate. And he was scared of the eventual outcome if she continued buying at the rate she'd been buying so far.

Often one person tends to be practical and frugal; the other an easy spender. Neither is necessarily right or wrong, but it's tough when they're stuck with solving their differences.

The only answer I see is continued respectful communication to seek answers that both will feel okay about. Admittedly, it's not easy. We need to keep shoulds and oughts out of it, and not allow tears and/or anger to interfere. We need to remember to stop the conversation when it gets too emotional, but to come back to it when feelings are again under control.

No solution has to be the final statement. It's good to say, "All right, let's try this way for a (month, quarter, year, whatever) and see how it works. If we don't like it we can always try another way."

I really believe that most of us are good people, not out

to cheat our partners. Our difficulties come mostly as we wrestle with what's fair and unfair in dealing with those we love. We can be most effective in finding compromises if we stay gentle and always honest.

Chapter 15

Till Death Do Us Part

The bride and groom heard the question, and they easily concurred, "I do." They meant it. Death! Lifetime! Commitment! Yeah!

But somewhere along the way they have begun to have misgivings and say, "I didn't know it was going to be like *this!*" They watch their friends get divorced and it sounds appealing. These are some of the things couples tell me:

"As I look back I don't think I was ever really in love with her. We dated, we liked each other. All our friends were getting married and we just kind of got swept away, too. It was the thing to do at the time."

"I was miserable living with my parents. He was a perfect way out."

"We had this great physical attraction, but after the honeymoon she lost interest in sex. I can't be expected to live in a sexless marriage, can I?"

"His mother dominates every thought he has. He's really married to *her.*"

"She just wants to party all the time. I want a wife who will have kids and cook. We ought to work together on our house, but she's never home."

"I thought I knew him, but I didn't. I still don't. He doesn't talk."

"Hey, I can tolerate anything but infidelity. I can't get the picture out of my mind of her with that other guy."

"If he'd quit drinking maybe we could make it work, but he won't."

"I've always come second to the kids."

"I've always come second to his job."

How much do we have to suffer before we're allowed to divorce? Are we *ever* justified? What if one wants out and the other doesn't?

There are so many options in life. Each choice we make has a price tag. Marriage is one of the best institutions around, but it has one of the highest costs. It is enormously expensive in terms of the energy necessary to keep it healthy.

There are at least two kinds of marriages that can work splendidly:

First is the old-fashioned arrangement that many Christians still believe is the best way. The husband is the head of the house, and he loves his wife as much as he loves himself. He takes as good care of her as he does his own body. He loves her as Christ loves the church. She is submissive to him, allows him to make the major decisions in their life, and she looks to him for guidance. Together they make a great combination. It works!

Second is the more modern arrangement that appeals to many couples today; the marriage of equal partners. Neither person is the "boss" or decision maker, but both make decisions equally. Neither is responsible for the other's well-being, but both love the other so much they nurture each other by choice. There is cooperation between them and respect for each other's rights. Together they make a great combination. It works!

I know people from both styles, and I believe both have the potential for success.

In the traditional Christian marriage the partners agree to follow this message: "Honor Christ by submitting to each other. You wives must submit to your husband's leadership in the same way you submit to the Lord. For a husband is in charge of his wife in the same way Christ is in charge of His body the Church. (He gave his very life to take care 'of it and be its Savior!) So you wives must willingly obey your husbands in everything, just as the church obeys Christ.

"And you husbands, show the same kind of love to your wives as Christ showed to the church when He died for her. That is how husbands should treat their wives, loving them as parts of themselves. For since a man and his wife are now one, a man is really doing himself a favor and loving himself when he loves his wife. A man must love his wife as part of himself; and the wife must see to it that she deeply respects her husband, obeying, praising and honoring him." (*The Living Bible,* Ephesians 5:21-25, 28, 33)

I know some marriages based on that teaching that are extremely happy. They're composed of special people who make God the center of their life together. The level of love required to insure the success of these marriages is exemplary, but because many people just can't seem to sustain it, we don't see good ones all around us.

A friend who has one of these marriages says, "There's no woman on earth who wouldn't follow a man who leads lovingly and gently."

By and large I agree with her. But it isn't easy for men to measure up to society's standards and still be the loving, gentle leaders their wives are looking for. They get caught up in building their careers, as a rule, and their primary focus becomes their jobs. Once wives feel like they're "playing second fiddle" to their husbands' work they lose some of their willingness to "obey, praise and honor."

I believe if a man truly did love his wife as part of himself, showing her the same kind of love Christ did when He died for the church, that wife would be the most loving, nurturing woman he could imagine.

But hell hath no fury as a woman scorned. And when women feel less important than their men's other interests, they can get downright nasty! Then we have a vicious circle. Both people want that loving closeness, but when they feel it lessening, they respond out of fear and often behave badly. They use anger or pouting, crying or withdrawing, drinking or overeating, or all kinds of efforts at manipulating to "get" the other person to love them again.

The more you distance yourself from me, the more I will distance myself from you, until we have a chicken-and-egg routine that often worsens as we blame each other for causing it.

"If he loved me I'd be the kind, nurturing, sexy wife he wants."

"If she acted lovingly I'd be there showing how much I love her."

Women want men to be those loving, gentle romantics we dream about. Yet, in truth, many men who have those qualities often seem too passive for us. If they're sensitive and communicative, and good at sharing feelings, they may not be the strong, aggressive men we admire as "successful." It's almost impossible for a man to be a combination of all those traits.

Men want women who are loving, gentle and romantic as well, but they often become annoyed if we're too dependent on them. They want us to be responsible for ourselves and not lean on them for everything. In fact, they often admire strong, assertive women even though they may be threatened by them at the same time. Women can't possibly be the perfect combination, either.

Marriages that last, then, will be between people who are wise enough to accept imperfection; those who can live and let live for the most part and not let their happiness be determined by their mate's behavior.

That takes us to the other type of marriage I know can be successful: the equality arrangement in which neither person is submissive to or responsible for the other one. But that's just as hard to carry off as the first kind we looked at.

In the relationship of equality, neither person has the right to expect to be "taken care of" by the other. Ideally we'll love each other enough to want to be loving and caring, and willing to share each other's burdens and joys. But if I'm unhappy, it's my fault.

Independent partners develop a lot of strength and gain continuing confidence as they strive to fill their own needs while also being helpmates to their spouses.

Sometimes, though, they lose a lot of the closeness they could have in a more interdependent relationship. Both people might become so fiercely independent that they're "married singles." They share the house, children and occasional meals, but most of their pleasure is found separately. The common bond weakens as they find themselves only good friends. There's still a lot of caring and respect between them, but it's not as strong a marriage as it could be.

No wonder we find ourselves discouraged when all the avenues are so fraught with difficulties. It takes two people who are really dedicated to having a good marriage if they're going to succeed.

Yesterday I saw a couple in my office who were already having doubts about their commitment, though they've been married just two years. (Many people don't make it past a year!)

"I think maybe it was a mistake we married in the first place," said Gary. "I feel like I've lost all my freedom. I'm 21, Leslie's 20, but our lives aren't any fun anymore. I still want to go out and party and she just wants to stay home. She doesn't want me to go alone. If I do she gets so upset I don't even enjoy myself."

Leslie added, "I can't trust him. He's already had an affair with another woman. He's cute, everyone loves him. But after a few drinks he loses his head. I'm very religious; don't drink; don't like to party. I want to have a baby, but he doesn't want the responsibility. He wants to run around like a young kid. I feel so sad, like the wonderful bond between us has been broken. I'm not sure I can ever love him like I used to."

My heart went out to both of them. They *are* young. I can't help wondering if they didn't marry in haste and youthful excitement, and maybe it *was* a poor decision. But now what do they do?

I always admit to clients that I have a bias toward helping people stay married if it can be worked out. Even if just *one* of the couple wants it, I try very hard to see if the problems can be resolved so they'll both choose to continue the marriage. But if one or both clearly doesn't want to work at it, I know I'm licked. Still, I try to find out how I *can* help them.

One of the questions I ask is whether or not they have spiritual convictions that marriage is forever. Some people say, "Yeah, I believe it's supposed to be permanent, but I know I can't live this way anymore. Next time I'll make a better choice. That one will be forever."

Some say they have no religious belief about m.
They see it as strictly societal.

Sometimes one believes one way and one the other.
Thank goodness it isn't my place to judge their beliefs.
Most of the time I'm able to view the situation objectively
and help them arrive at whatever resolution seems the
best to them. But it's a lot harder when there are children
who will be hurt if the marriage dissolves. On the other
hand, staying together "for the sake of the children" isn't
always the best thing, either. Children don't gain much
stability in a home filled with anger and resentment.

The whole question of commitment confuses me. I
confess that to my clients. I'm willing to help them untan-
gle feelings and problems. I will be the calm, objective
"outsider" who looks for untried solutions and attempts
to keep the atmosphere respectful and productive. But
I'm glad I'm not the one who has to decide whether or
not the marriage should continue; that's their responsibility.

There seem to be three possible states of married life.
The worst is full of unhappiness, anger, hurt, lack of communication and closeness. It's the most likely to end in
divorce.

In the middle group, the partners have sunk into a kind
of apathy, resigning themselves to a mediocre, ordinary
but very lackluster relationship. It might last for years, but
neither person will enjoy it much.

The best, of course, is that of bliss. A supreme kind of
joy that shows in both people's faces when they see each
other or even talk about each other. It's the state most of
us think we're getting when we marry, but it's the most
elusive. Many of us get to experience it only for a year or
two in the beginning.

Is it ever too late to achieve that state? *I* don't think so.

No matter how many times we've been hurt by each other, we always have the capacity to try again.

Stockbrokers get shrewder at handling investments as they put in year after year of working at the skill. Photographers become adept at choosing shutter speeds as they take more and more pictures. Gardeners become both scientists and artists through their years of dealing with aphids and fertilizers. Chefs produce better epicurean dishes, beauticians create better haircuts and musicians perform ever more beautifully.

We can get better at anything if we practice it. So in spite of thousands of disappointments and setbacks in our marriage, we always have the ability to improve our skills in relating to each other.

One good way to start (or continue) is marriage counseling. For most of us that seems like a scary thing to do. We hate to admit we could use help in dealing with what "should" be something we can handle ourselves.

I remember the first time Larry and I agreed we might benefit from counseling. I made the appointment, then canceled it. I made it again, and canceled it again. Each time we were a couple of days away from the meeting, we talked each other out of going. "It'll be all right; we can solve this alone," we told ourselves.

That's pretty standard behavior for most of us. That first session is a hard hurdle to cross. But it's worth it!

If you haven't a clue which counselor to call and you have the courage to share with a friend that you're considering counseling, you'll find recommendations coming out of the woodwork. *Everybody's* been to counseling, it seems. When someone glows as he talks about the counselor who helped him and his wife, take him seriously. He wouldn't be recommending someone who left him lukewarm.

You have a right to know what kind of credibility a counselor has. What level of education? In some states, anyone can be a counselor just by hanging out a shingle. Look for someone trained at no less than a Master's level, or with training from a religious facility you know and trust.

Look them up in The Yellow Pages (usually under "Marriage Counselors") and ask about fees. Don't be embarrassed. It's a perfectly acceptable question, especially in this relationship where honesty is valued. You can almost always find a counselor who's willing to work with you if you have trouble paying all at once.

Many therapists charge a sliding fee scale. Many medical insurance plans pay for at least a portion of mental health and/or marriage counseling.

Feel free to ask about affiliations. It's reassuring to know your therapist belongs to some associations that demand certain standards be met by their members. One major one is the American Association for Marriage and Family Therapy. The National Academy of Certified Clinical Mental Health Counselors is another reputable one, as are the National Board for Certified Counselors and the American Association for Counseling and Development.

There are a few psychiatrists who do marriage counseling, but most of them refer patients to counselors. Look for letters: Ph.D., M.Ed., Ed.D., M.A., or M.S.W., all indicating graduate degrees.

When you choose a counselor, give yourself permission to try one session. It's very important to find someone with whom you feel comfortable. If you don't, by all means don't go back. There are so many styles of counselors, you can find one with whom you'll relate well. You might need to shop around and try two or three in order to settle on the one who seems helpful and insightful, as well as comfortable. Look for someone who obviously understands you.

It's important to be honest. The counseling process will be much less lengthy and costly if everything that's said is the truth. A therapist may be fooled by a client's lies, but the problems can't possibly be solved, so it's a waste of time and money not to be honest.

You might be slightly nervous at first, but that will disappear as you begin feeling at home. Anything we do for the first time often causes a little anxiety in the beginning.

Thank goodness the days are almost gone when there was a stigma attached to counseling. People used to think of it as something only crazy people needed. Now, it's not only acceptable, there's a certain amount of pride evident in many people who talk openly about their therapy.

I look at it much like taking a class. We're learning new information in a very comfortable "classroom" where the teacher is focusing all his or her energy on only us. It's wonderful! We can ask all the questions we want, and they'll always be answered with respect and understanding. It's private; no one laughs or makes fun of us, and we feel more acceptance there than almost anywhere else. Not only that, all three of us are there with a common objective: To make this couple happier! Can you beat that for a great way to spend an hour?

One important bit of advice: Do what the counselor suggests, as far as homework. Sometimes couples come back week after week admitting a little sheepishly that they didn't have time to talk to each other. You don't want to waste your money on advice designed to help you if you're going to disregard it.

Larry and I have had marriage counseling with five different counselors in our 36 years together. We've benefited more from some than others, but both of us agree each one has given us something positive with which to work. We still quote lines from all five counselors. And they'd probably be pleased to know how much they live on in our lives.

Being both a counselor and a counselee, I know how it feels to risk. People often look embarrassed and ask, "This will be confidential, won't it?"

I can't emphasize enough that any reputable counselor is aware of the need for confidentiality. For counselors to slip and reveal anything would be risking their entire reputation and, therefore, their livelihood. You don't dare. Feel perfectly confident that your secrets won't leave the room.

The funny thing is, your secrets are way more common than you may think. There isn't any *new* behavior in this world. The things you're saying have been said before, probably many times over. Human beings make the same mistakes, have the same feelings and thoughts and doubts that human beings have always had and will continue having. Your counselor won't be shocked.

What if you want to get counseling and your partner refuses? Go anyway. While it is much quicker and easier to help a marriage improve if both parties participate in counseling, a lot can be accomplished with only one. As you learn what you're doing wrong and make some changes, it will affect your mate's thoughts and feelings, and perhaps even behavior.

Maybe you think you're not doing anything wrong. But even if your mate is 99 percent responsible for all the problems of the marriage, we can still look at the one percent that's yours. It's amazing what can be accomplished by changing even one percent of your behavior.

And, as you progress in counseling and your spouse begins to see changes, she or he may decide to give it a try as well. This is even more likely to happen if we don't hammer the subject to death. Have you ever been around a person who is so excited about a new religion or program that he drives you away? You cringe when you see him approaching, knowing you're going to get another sales pitch about why you should switch churches or go to a health-food lecture or take a personal-growth seminar. The harder he tries to get you to go, the more determined you are to resist.

On the other hand, if you see an unhappy person begin to get happier, you wonder why. You watch to see if it will continue. If it does, you begin to want some of whatever it is that seems so effective.

By going alone to a counselor you're telling your mate, in effect, "I'm really unhappy. I can't seem to resolve my problems, so I'm going for help. I'd love to have you join me, but I'm going even if you don't. If you ever want to come along, you're welcome . . . and I'll be delighted!"

What if you're living in an impossible situation that you can't cope with anymore, but your mate refuses to discuss it, get help or make any changes? How long must you live that way?

Most of us need help in that situation. If not a counselor (which would be my first recommendation), then a good friend, family member, or someone at your church or synagogue. Sometimes you're so close to a situation you lose perspective and become frozen; miserable and unable to move in any productive kind of way.

A typical example is the husband or wife of an alcoholic or drug addict. It becomes a rotten way to live, affecting every aspect of the family. The problem touches all the lives in a sad, destructive way, sometimes continuing for years because no one knows quite what to do.

I can't say enough good things about Al-Anon, an organization designed just for that situation. If you go, you'll learn now to handle everything. You hear other people share their experiences and it's like hearing your own family talking. You may realize for the first time you're not alone—millions of people are in the same boat. And now you have their accumulated experience and wisdom to draw from. Many people are reluctant to go for fear of being seen and recognized, but everyone there has someone in their lives who's into some addictive behavior. You'll probably make some friends there who will become very close to you, friends you'll treasure. Look for Al-Anon in your Yellow Pages under "Alcoholism Treatment."

You don't have to live in a wretched situation. But you may need help to discover some of the options you get to consider in finding relief.

No matter what problem you have with a mate, the advice is the same. Get some outside help. No one has to put up with abuse; verbal, physical or sexual. Nor should our children have to endure it.

Commitment to marriage does not mean we have to stay stuck in a rotten situation, but we may need help in getting ourselves un-stuck.

Some people decide to separate. They've talked themselves blue, trying to get a spouse to acknowledge a problem, but it seems to fall on deaf ears. Finally they know they're licked, and they tell their partners something like this:

"I'm defeated. I've hurt so much for so long, and I haven't been able to get any help from you in dealing with our problems. I can't do it alone. I'm too discouraged to keep trying because I know you don't think there's a problem . . . and I can't change you. I need to take care of myself, though. I'm going to start looking for an apartment."

If you say it, mean it. Don't use it as manipulation. Do it only when you've tried every avenue for improving the situation and come to nothing but dead ends.

Sadly, a disinterested mate often sits up and takes notice when it's too late. I wish I had a nickel for every marriage I've seen in that last fatal stage, when either the wife or the husband is throwing in the towel. Usually the more submissive party has swallowed a lot of anger for some years and now has suddenly become assertive and won't take any more.

Too many times the marriage could have been saved if it had been attended to earlier. If your partner is telling you there's a problem in the marriage, please *believe it!* If one person has a problem, both people have and it needs to be addressed.

Another strong conviction I have about leaving a marriage is this: Falling in love with another person is the wrong reason for leaving. In that euphoric state we're back to the insanity we felt for our prince or princess in the beginning. I own a marble paperweight on which is printed, "A person in love is a very poor judge of character." I might add that a person in love is a poor judge of almost everything, so that's certainly not the right time to get a divorce.

One comment I hear from troubled spouses is, "You know, as I've thought about it over the years, I think I could have made my first marriage work if I'd been willing to work at it. The other grass is always greener."

When you leave a partner for his imperfections and marry another, you have to cope with different imperfections. You could go through a lot of partners that way. It's easier to keep working on the one we've got.

Nevertheless I do recognize the fact that some marriages were a great mistake in the first place. I sometimes heave a great sigh of relief when the couples agree to end it. It's not so hard to watch a divorce when both people want out.

It's very difficult when only one does. The person who's left really needs help to deal with all the grief he or she will be going through; the same stages of grief you go through in losing someone to death (denial, bargaining, anger, depression and finally acceptance).

The person leaving generally has been planning to exit for some time and sees the step as a positive one, one that's necessary to relieve pain. The other faces a tremendous shock, filled with profound hurt and anger. That person needs a lot of encouragement in order to move toward acceptance.

I had a client named Bill who was in just that position.

He was so devastated by the loss of his marriage that he became depressed and finally suicidal. One evening he swallowed a lot of pills and lay down to die.

"As I was beginning to feel a numbness throughout my body I got frightened," he recounted later. "I realized I didn't want to give up this life. Suddenly I knew how much I wanted to live, and I was so numb and fuzzy I could hardly pick up the phone. I did manage to, by the grace of God, and somehow got an operator who sent out the paramedics." He was rushed to the hospital and released a few days later.

When I saw him next, he was a different man. The depression was gone and he was obviously ready to live life again. In those moments of near-death he'd turned a corner and decided to embrace the future positively. From then on our therapy was easy.

At the end of his last session he said, "If there's ever anyone you think I could help, please call me. I think I could understand someone who feels the way I felt, and I'd be glad to do whatever I could."

Several months later I met Anne, a sad, sweet lady who was struggling with her own depression. We worked together for a while, and I told her about Bill who had offered a kind ear to anyone in that position. She was dubious, but decided to meet him for coffee.

A year later they invited me to their wedding. Every now and then when I run into them, they're still holding hands. Those two give me goose bumps, they're so happy, and they're proof that life can always be even happier than it was before. Being left by a spouse is not the end of the world.

People have amazing ability to adjust. We never have to *stay* unhappy.

Still, many divorces I've seen wouldn't have to have happened if the people involved knew a little more about improving marriage instead of junking it. Sometimes I think it's almost contagious; seeing friends divorce each other makes it seem more and more acceptable. It becomes simpler to quit working on the discouraging relationship and opt for what seems like a better solution: just get out.

We've gotten used to fast foods, whipping into drive-in lanes for a quick-fix of burger, fries and drink slid across the counter in less than two minutes. But we all know that a sumptuous dinner tastes a lot better, lasts longer and is ever so much more nutritious. It takes longer to fix and to eat, but the overall reward is one most of us would choose any day over a quickie-burger.

A lifetime marriage on which we spend time and energy is going to be the most satisfying, sumptuous feast we could want, well worth the work it takes.

I'm picturing two friends of ours who are in their "golden years." Retired and enjoying life thoroughly, they had us over for dinner one night and were proudly showing us around their home. We admired a fireplace, and the woman said, "We love it. We use it a lot, all winter. Sometimes we make love right here on the rug in the firelight," and they looked fondly at each other.

I was moved at the love I saw in their eves, and hoped I would feel as loving toward Larry when we are their age.

I know I *can,* but not unless I keep trying. There are still those times when I don't feel any noticeable love for him; in fact, I don't even much *like* him. I've even thought occasionally, "I don't want to put up with this anymore. Maybe I oughta get me a little townhouse and live there all by myself."

But I know, too, it's a temporary stage, and I'll get over it. Sometimes I've prayed, "Help me love him more." And sometimes even, "Help me *want* to love him more," when I've been really put off.

It no longer alarms me when I feel that hostility, because I always end up loving him again. I reflect on those times and liken my attitude to a sulky kid who's all bent out of shape because the cookies are gone.

I can dig my toes into the ground and feel self-pity if I want. Or complain to all the neighbors that the cookie jar is bare. I might even choose to lash out at someone in the house that he should provide me with my cookie supply.

But one of the advantages of being grown up is resourcefulness in providing my own cookies. I can bake them or buy them, but it's up to me to keep my supply replenished.

If I'm unhappy, *I* am the one to see about it. When I get sufficiently miserable with my life I can say, "I don't have to put up with this kind of behavior from myself anymore," and set about finding solutions.

Most of us married for the wrong reasons: romantic excitement and someone to take care of us, filling our every need. But if we keep working at it, we'll probably end up being married for the *right* reasons.

Having someone in life who knows us better than anyone else. Someone who tolerates our bad behavior in exchange for the right to exhibit some as well. Someone we can nurture and care about, but not feel responsible for. A person to hug. A driver to provide the sound of a familiar car coming home. A partner to share both the pleasure and the pain of raising children. And the special pride of hearing a grandchild begin to talk. Not a perfect person who might intimidate us by contrast, but an ordinary velveteen-rabbit-type person who grows more loveable with all the years of pummeling that life dishes out. A sharer of thousands of memories and in-house jokes that guarantee a smile. Eyes to meet across a room that understand, "I want to go home." A friend to cry with. Someone with whom to make love on the rug by the fireplace when we're old. Tenderly.

Final Thanks

People often ask, "Uh . . . how does Larry feel about your honesty in these books? I mean, you're pretty open, don't you think?"

I am. And so is Larry. Over the years we've realized we're really much like everybody else, so there's not a lot to hide. Still, I would not have let a chapter go to press without his approval. He read each one as I finished it and made encouraging comments all along the way. He's also carted hundreds of boxes of books to seminars and post offices. How I value his constant support!

Laurie takes my hastily typed copy and edits it skillfully, bringing clarity and order to my jumbled first draft. I couldn't produce a book without her advice, professional expertise and enthusiasm.

Lisa shoots great pictures for the back covers of my books. Also, she and I trade theories and thoughts by the hour, and much of my writing is inspired by her fresh, creative thinking.

Ginger generously gave me the courage to be honest as I struggled with the chapter on in-laws. I'm thankful for the healing and growth she's helped me achieve.

Lindsay and Lyle have yet to read one of my books. "We know everything you have to say, Mom," they explain. But they compliment my pork chops and dumplings.

A Gift For You

There's a message I give newlyweds in the form of a poem I wrote about the importance of communication. I enclose this poem in a box with two silver goblets, an unusual wedding gift. You have my permission to copy the poem if you'd like to encourage conversation, too.

Dear _____ and _____,

These goblets are magic, as you will attest
When you've used them and found they bring out the best
Of the love that's between you: a wonderful thing!
It's precious and endless, like your wedding ring.

Here's how they work: When you two have a fight,
Whether it's small or lasts long in the night,
Either can get out the goblets and pour
Some beverage for drinking "an end to the war."

Just offer the goblet, a gesture of peace.
The message implies, "Let's let anger cease."
"To us!" you both say as you toast one another.
You sip and you listen and you talk to each other.

Often the magic works quickly and well,
And soon the solution is clear as a bell.
But when the cup's empty, if things aren't okay,
Just pour you some more and keep chatting away.

If you talk long enough in a kind, gentle way,
The problem may solve itself that very day.
The magic continues as long as you each
Converse with respect. Understanding you'll reach.

But if, in the course of sipping and talking,
Either starts crying or shouting or walking,
Then stop for a while. It might be the best
To bring it up later when it's had a rest.

You can drink from them anytime, happy or sad,
But the magic is strongest when feelings are bad.
With enough conversation these goblets assure
That your life will be happy. Your love will endure!

Lee Schnebly

Recommended Books

Bayard, Robert and Bayard, Jean, *How To Deal With Your Acting Up Teenager,* The Accord Press, 1981

Beecher, Marguerite and Beecher, Willard, *Beyond Success And Failure,* The Julian Press, Inc., 1986

Beecher, Marguerite and Beecher, Willard, *Parents On The Run,* Cevorss and Co., 1983

Carnes, Patrick, *Out Of The Shadows,* Compcare Publications, *1983*

Collins, Vincent, *Me, Myself And You,* Abbey Press, 1974

Diets, Bob, *Life After Loss,* Fisher Books, 1988

Dinkmeyer, Don and McKay, Gary, *Systematic Training for Effective Parenting,* American Guidance Service, 1976

Dobson, James, *Love Must Be Tough,* Word Books, 1983

Dreikurs, Rudolph and Soltz, Vickie, *Children: The Challenge,* Hawthorne Books, 1964 ·

Dyer, Wayne, *Your Erroneous Zones,* Avon, 1976

Ellis, Albert and Harper, Robert, *A New Guide To Rational Living,* 1975

Fontenelle, Don, *How to Live with Your Children,* Fisher Books, 1988

Ford, Edward, *Why Marriage?,* Argus, 1974

Glasser, William, *Positive Addiction*, Harper & Row, 1985

Gordon, Thomas, *Parent Effectiveness Training*, New American Library, 1970

Guhl, Beverly and Fontenelle, Don, *Purrfect Parenting*, Fisher Books, 1987

Jampolsky, Gerald, *Love is Letting Go of Fear*, Bantam, 1979

Kennedy, Eugene, *A Time For Love*, Doubleday, 1970

Leman, Kevin, *Making Children Mind Without Losing Yours*, Dell, 1987

Lerner, Harriet Goldhor, *The Dance Of Anger*, Perennial Library, Harper & Row, 1985

Powell, John, *The Secret Of Staying In Love*, Argus, 1974

Schnebly, Lee, *Do It Yourself Happiness*, Fisher Books, 1988

Schnebly, Lee, *Out Of Apples?*, Fisher Books, 1988

Schneider, Jennifer, *Back From Betrayal*, Harper & Row, 1988

Segal, Julius, *A Child's Journey*, McGraw Hill, 1978

Viscott, David, *How To Live With Another Person*, Pocket Books, 1974

Walton, Francis X. and Powers, Robert, *Winning Children Over*, Practical Psychology Associates, 1974

Walton, Francis X., *Winning Teenagers Over In Home And School*, Adlerian Child Care Books, 1980

Index